Harvesting Financial Prosperity

Brent M. Johnson

Book cover by Rob Williams

Edition 1 2024

Table of Contents

Preface

I aim to make you a better-educated financial services client for all your investment, insurance, and financial planning requirements and make you a more informed decision-maker about investments, insurance, financial planning, & estate planning products.

I was an MBA, Chartered Financial Analyst, CFP, and investment and insurance licensed Financial Advisor for Merrill Lynch, Guardian Life Insurance, and Woodbury. I spent twelve years as a Financial Advisor, primarily as a portfolio manager for retirement/investment account clients. I earned above average returns every year, and lost very little money in market downturns, because of my superior risk management.

I have purchased $55 million worth of bonds and stocks, about $5 million in annuities, and several million in alternative investments. So I know what I am talking about. I performed very well for my clients. This book reveals my thinking and practices, so you can earn superior returns also. Much of that depends on your advisor, their training, their firm, your relationship with the advisor and the firm, and whether your advisor is accountable for their results.

I hope to help you hold your advisor accountable, earn above average returns, and ,avoid conflicts with your advisory firms and advisors and steer you to better relationships with firms, advisors, and insurance agents. I desire that your relationship with your advisor serves your interests. I have found when there is a mature relationship and transparency between advisors and investors, the relationship is much more fruitful for both parties.

This book offers my experience and advice, what I learned about firms, advisors, products, and clients. This book can make you a more informed, aware investor and purchaser of financial services and help you understand who is best qualified to offer which products. And also, I will set your expectations in what you should expect from an advisor who manages or oversees your investments.

Chapter One

KEY INVESTMENT ELEMENTS

This chapter begins with explaining some key aspects of investing: risk management, fundamental and technical analysis, asset allocation, portfolio diversification, behavioral finance, investor psychology, alternative investments, and lay the groundwork for further discussion about investments, and how it is done with advisors and firms, which we will discuss in Chapter two.

Risk Management

What is risk management? It is a strategy to identify, analyze, and mitigate risk and minimize the uncertainty of returns from the investment. It varies by the type of investment, between cash, bonds, stocks, and real estate, and is usually specific to the asset. Every investment has risk: investors cannot separate the risk and return from any investment: those two concepts are inseparable.

The most common measure of risk in investing is using the standard deviation of the investment's returns, a measure of dispersion around the mean [central tendency].

For example, the risk with cash is that there is a cost to liquidity: investment returns [cash flow] could be earned that are higher than holding cash. But there is also the risk that the investment made will be lost. So, balancing risk and reward is very important.

A portfolio manager with cash will likely make investment choices based on time horizon, credit quality, and other investing opportunities. If a decision has been made to invest cash, it is likely to be determined by credit quality.

The risk in longer-term bonds, with maturities of 10-30 years, is that interest rates rise and bond values decline, resulting in investment losses. The most common way to reduce risk in bond investing is a ladder, staggering the maturities of bonds. This strategy can increase cash returns without a dramatic risk increase, for example, in one to five-year bonds. For example, if interest rates are decreasing, a decision may be made for Treasury bonds vs. corporate bonds for safety, and in assessing risk, the portfolio manager sees the difference in returns between Treasuries and Corporate bonds do not compensate for the increased risk in Corporate bonds.

What is interest rate risk? It is the risk that fixed-income investments, such as cash and bonds, have lower returns, either through lower coupons (income) being offered as interest rates rise, which lowers the investor's return. Interest rate risk may be reduced by diversifying the maturity of bonds, reducing the maturity of bonds, or by buying derivatives [such as options or futures], reducing the risk of increasing interest rates. Additionally, bonds have default risk. Most investors consider US Treasury bonds to have near zero default risk.

The risk of investing in stocks is that the returns from investing, dividends, and rising stock prices have a much higher standard deviation than bonds. That is why the returns are higher, but losses may be more common, depending upon the equity investments chosen.

The investor's risk tolerance likely drives decisions between equity choices. For example, a moderate investor might not invest in small-capitalization stocks [or invest a small % of assets in them], thus an asset allocation strategy of reducing risk.

Another method of reducing risk in stocks, beyond diversifying by size [large-mid-small-capitalization] and between value and growth, and geography [international vs. USA], would be **using options and futures**, such as selling calls to generate more income, a risk-reducing strategy, or buying calls on stocks that are undervalued, increasing risk and adding concentration.

The risks of investing in real estate are decreases in cash flow, credit quality, and from lower saleability [the ability to convert the investment to cash], decreases in cash flow resulting in reduced investment value, and delays in sales that may cause substantial decreases in returns and investment value.

For example, a timber investment requires timely planting and harvesting of trees, selling and contracting when prices are rising, not falling, and possibly liquidating properties to investors with longer time horizons [more extended investment holding pattern] than the current investors. Timber investors may diversify their holdings by the product, the type of trees grown, and the time it takes to grow certain trees [shortening or lengthening the investment holding period], along with geographic diversification.

Another type of risk is currency risk: a portfolio manager may have limits on holding only a % of assets in a specific currency. Let's say a $1 billion bond fund's portfolio manager can only invest 40% in the USD [US dollar]. They may diversify the currency risk by using derivatives, effectively reducing the risk of a particular currency.

Risk management strategies
Investopedia has a list of the most common investment risk strategiess:

1. **Avoidance:** Manage your risk is by avoiding it altogether, cutting out volatility and risk, choosing the safest assets with fewer risks.

2. **Retention:** Accepting risks and acknowledging that they come with the territory. This strategy assumes that the investor is being compensated for assuming additional risk.

3. **Sharing:** Involves two or more parties taking on an agreed-upon portion of the risk. For instance, reinsurers cover risks that insurance companies can't handle independently.

4. **Transferring:** Risks can be passed on from one party to another. For instance, health insurance involves passing on the risk of coverage from you to your insurer as long as you pay premiums.

5. **Loss Prevention and Reduction:** Find ways to minimize your losses by preventing them from spreading to other areas. Diversification may be a way for investors to reduce their losses.[1]

Types of Research: Fundamental and Technical

What is the fundamental analysis of investments? It means investment research that looks at a company's financial statements, the income statement for income and expenses, the balance sheet to review assets, liabilities, and equity, and the cash flow statement to understand the company's operations on a cash basis.

Bond investors would analyze the company for its credit rating and ability to pay interest, while equity investors would look for earnings growth and capital appreciation of the common shares. Preferred stock investors would look for the ability to pay interest on its stock, before dividends are paid to common stock holders.

Stock research can be fundamental, technical, or a mix of the two. At Merrill Lynch, I read economic, sector, and company reports, usually a mix of fundamental and technical analysis. The analyst who drafted the

---

[1] Investopedia website, search dated February 4, 2024, https://www.investopedia.com/terms/r/riskmanagement.asp

report usually was an expert in that industry and knew the trends in that industry. The report summarized what trends were taking place now, what companies were performing well [and placed on a buy list], and what companies were performing poorly and [placed on a sell list].

So, what is technical analysis? Technical analysis looks for trends in sectors, companies, etc., through charts, usually based on sector performance, company performance, price and volume data, etc. You can recognize trends and information summarized in charts faster, and is more straightforward than seeing the data from spreadsheets.

Technical analysis can include bond or equity charts and compare their performance. I found technical analysis especially helpful in the short term, when trends change, when equity markets sputter and fight to achieve gains, when interest rates rise,and when many S&P 500 companies report earnings below expectations. Using charts can be helpful when choosing between equity positions for adding to your. investment portfolio.

I reviewed investment candidate companies weekly, using some fundamental analysis like Earnings per share [EPS] and stock prices, for capital appreciation in the last quarter and in the previous year or two.

Charts make this easy, especially when you have software programmed to give you charts of major market indices, such as the S&P 500 , the Nasdaq 100, and mid-cap indices. Other charts would analyze the best performing sectors and companies within those sectors, along with sectors not performing, and companies within those sectors. Usually, this analysis confirmed there were profits to be taken from long-term positions and reinvested in better performing sectors and companies. Advisors always need to know what are the best performing bonds and equities now, and what are lagging sectors and companies.

Both fundamental and technical analysis are helpful tools in your toolbox. Most of the time, I used both, depending on whether I was stock picking or identifying trends in equity markets and sectors, or having investment meetings with clients to discuss their investment performance.

Asset Allocation and Diversification

How does Asset Allocation and Diversification work for investors? Each of your investments [cash, bonds, stocks, alternative investments] has an industry standard to measure the returns. So, agree with your financial advisor in advance on the return standards for each asset you own, then measure your returns with those standards every month, quarter, and year.

Then, you will know what investments are performing well and which are underperforming, and then develop strategies to increase returns. This process is fundamental to portfolio management.

You must measure your returns against agreed-upon standards for each asset in your investment portfolio before you will have any accountability from your advisor.

In my experience as a financial advisor, until this is done, there is no accountability. I learned to establish clear investment goals and benchmarks right away with each client, which usually led to firing underperforming advisors and increased assets for me. I am not bragging; I am just saying that an advisor who consistently underperforms should lose assets, and advisors who perform well and overperform deserve to manage more assets.

So what is Asset Allocation? It is allocating investment dollars to specific investments. For example, the most common Asset Allocation is choosing how much investment dollars go to cash, bonds, or stocks/equities, for a portfolio, say of $1.5 million. A common allocation for a moderate risk tolerance investor [more about investment risk tolerance later], would be:

1. Cash: 10%, or $150,000.

2. Bonds: 40%, or $600,000.

3. Stocks/equities: 50%, or $750,000.

The goal in asset allocation is to balance risk and reward. Cash does not have significant capital appreciation: but it bears little risk of loss sitting in most banks. However, liquidity is helpful when bond and equity market values appreciate, when additional funds can be invested to increase returns. Bonds usually earn more than cash, but bear more investment risk. Conservative investors buy more Treasury bonds than Corporate bonds, and more investment grade Corporate bonds than high yield bonds. Equities have the most risk of these three assets, but can offer the highest return on investment.

Diversification is the result from asset allocation: that by dividing investment dollars between cash, stocks, and bonds [and possibly alternative investments] and further by investing among different categories of cash, stocks [Large-mid-small-cap and between value and growth in each category], and bonds [Treasuries vs Corporate vs Munich], that risk can be minimized in each category while earning the highest reward possible based upon the risks the investor wants to assume: not too much risk nor too little reward. So, by investing cash in Treasury securities, laddered with maturities of 1-3 years, risk is reduced and the reward is above that earned in Certificates of Deposit and money market accounts.

By investing in Treasury bonds with maturities of 5-10 years, and Corporate bonds of 3-12 years, the investor can choose the risk return desired, and earn higher returns than cash. And by investing in equities, investors can seek higher returns than bonds, and choose the amount of risk assumed, by choosing among equity investments.

For example, where an aggressive investor, who seeks the highest equity returns, would choose to invest in small cap stocks, and international equities in high growth economies, a conservative investor, with the lowest risk profile, would primarily invest in large cap stocks, and dividend paying stocks, and not have the risk tolerance for the other investments made by the aggressive investor, specifically, small cap stocks, and international equities.

The moderate investor risk tolerance would be middle ground, allowing for some small-cap, mid-cap, and large-capitalization stocks, with smaller allocations to higher risk small cap stocks, and investing in value and growth among the large-, mid-, and small-capitalization allocations.

The key principle in diversification is that the risk and returns of each asset class are unique, and uncorrelated with other asset classes [cash, bonds, stocks, alternative assets]. Correlation is a statistical measure: correlation can be calculated between asset classes. Simply stated, It means that assets risk and returns behave fundamentally different and independently from each other.

Behavioral Finance

What is behavioral finance? It is a subfield of behavioral economics, which asserts that investors have psychological influences upon their actions in financial markets, and that some of these actions are biased. These behaviors can explain certain market anomalies, such as market panics or euphoria, where investors sell out of fear or buy out of greed, and explain that markets can be under-priced, or over-priced at any time.

Behavioral finance typically encompasses five main concepts:

1. **Mental accounting:** Mental accounting refers to the propensity for people to allocate money for specific purposes.

2. **Herd behavior:** Herd behavior states that people tend to mimic the financial behaviors of the majority of the herd. Herding is notorious in the stock market as the cause behind dramatic rallies and sell-offs.

3. **Emotional gap:** The emotional gap refers to decision-making based on extreme emotions or emotional strains such as anxiety, anger, fear, or excitement. Oftentimes, emotions are a key reason why people do not make rational choices.

4. **Anchoring**: Anchoring refers to attaching a spending level to a certain reference. Examples may include spending consistently based on a budget level or rationalizing spending based on different satisfaction utilities.

5. **Self-attribution**: Self-attribution refers to a tendency to make choices based on overconfidence in one's own knowledge or skill. Self-attribution usually stems from an intrinsic knack in a particular area. Within this category, individuals tend to rank their knowledge higher than others, even when it objectively falls short.[2]

Breaking down biases further, many individual biases and tendencies have been identified for behavioral finance analysis. Some of these include:

---

[2] Investopedia website, February 3, 2024, see https://www.investopedia.com/terms/b/behavioralfinance.asp

1. **Confirmation bias** is when investors have a bias toward accepting information that confirms their already-held belief in an investment. If information surfaces, investors accept it readily to confirm that they're correct about their investment decision—even if the information is flawed.

2. **Experiential bias** occurs when investors' memory of recent events makes them biased or leads them to believe that the event is far more likely to occur again. For this reason, it is also known as recency bias or availability bias. For example, the financial crisis in 2008 and 2009 led many investors to exit the stock market, and expected more economic hardship in the coming years. The experience of this negative event increased their bias or likelihood that the event could reoccur. In reality, the economy recovered, and the market bounced back in the years to follow.

3. **Loss aversion** is when investors place a greater weighting on avoiding losses vs. seeking market gains. These investors lassign a higher priority to avoiding losses than making investment gains, seeking higher rewards payout in the market to compensate for losses, and may avoid risk. The disposition effect occurs when investors sell their winners and hang onto their losers. The flaw in disposition bias is that the performance of the investment is tied to the entry price for the investor. Here the investor gauges the performance of their investment based on their individual entry price disregarding fundamentals or attributes of the investment.

4. **Familiarity bias** is where investors nvest in what they know: for example, in domestic companies or locally owned investments. As a result, investors are not diversified across multiple sectors and types of investments, which can reduce risk. Investors tend to go with investments that they have a history or have familiarity with.

Common resistance to diversification is not investing in unfamiliar industries, geographies, etc,[3]

Advisors have biases also. Their biases are their professional knowledge, their experiences in markets, both good and bad, and what they perceive as their greatest professional strengths, such as discerning equity markets.

Due to investing being their job, many FAs [financial advisors] have difficulties admitting a mistake when investment dollars are lost: they make excuses; the market did not act rationally; they bought too early or sold too late, etc. I have heard endless explanations from both advisors and clients as to why they lost money. Every person has biases. It is more honest to recognize them, and invest by research and rationality than by your emotions. But be honest about your emotions, when they are driving your actions.

Remember that cognitive biases are systematic errors in thinking, that will hinder your investing. It is more honest to discover them, in yourself and your advisor, than to claim that you don't have them. Everyone has biases about investing. Every person has emotions about investing.

One bias I found common in the investment world, I call the "smartest man syndrome." This can be a bias of advisors or clients, especially with contrarian thinkers. Advisors get this when they think they are the only one who can see market trends, gain insights from economic data, or find companies that no-one else can see that this is a great investment. And clients get this when they read research, or gain some intuition, or think they are the only ones who recognize that a company in an industry they have some knowledge of, is the best investment since sliced bread. I have found this bias working in me also. Everyone is prone to this

---

[3] Investopedia website, search from February 3,2024, per https://www.investopedia.com/terms/b/behavioralfinance.asp

syndrome. Realize now that you may be smart, but you are not the smartest investor who ever lived, and that others are smart too. You may have a serious hunch, but it will be recognized by other market participants shortly.

Investor Psychology

Investor psychology is the study of the emotional and cognitive factors that influence the decision-making process of investors. It refers to the mental and emotional factors that influence an investor's decision-making process when it comes to buying, holding, or selling investments. This includes a range of cognitive biases and emotions that can impact an investor's perceptions, attitudes, and behaviors. Understanding investor psychology is crucial for making informed investment decisions and avoiding common pitfalls.[4]

Alternative investments

What are alternative investments? These investments are investments that the risk and returns are not closely correlated with other investments, such as cash, bonds, and equities. Alternative investments can include futures, derivatives such as options, private equity, venture capital hedge funds, managed futures, commodities, art and antiques.

Just to be clear: they are alternative investments because their risk and returns characteristics vary statistically from other assets classes, such as cash, bonds, and equities.

I believe these investments help investors diversify risk, add income, and fight inflation. I recommended oil and gas properties and timber investments to my clients. These investments assist investors when choices, such as bonds and equities, hold more risk due to massive amounts of printed money in the past ten years in the US, inflation, and

---

[4] Per Google search, February 4, 2024, see https://www.financestrategists.com/wealth-management/investor-psychology/

at least in 2023, a rising interest rate environment, making it more difficult to make money with bonds, and with more risk in equities.

And when it is costly to hold cash [liquidity] and risk is high in bond and equity markets, what do you do? In this investment environment, I would place investors with moderate risk tolerance in alternative investments, such as oil and gas, especially those that produce higher levels of income that the bonds and stocks in their current investment portfolios. We will discuss alternative investments more as we go forward.

Here are some recommendations that you can use to build your wealth now:

1. **Start saving**. See if you can cut expenses or grow your income. Save in your 401k at work if you have one, or start an IRA on your own. Best to do a ROTH IRA. You don't get a tax deduction, but you minimize taxes on the distributions.

2. **Continue saving**. Set annual savings goals, what % of your income, and where you will do this, preferably savings and investment accounts.

3. **Start learning about investments**. Invest only in what you know and understand. Read about investments. If you already have an advisor, always recognize the risk and the rate of return on all your investment assets.If you have $100,000 or more saved and have home insurance, **hire an advisor** to review your insurance plan and make recommendations on your investments.

4. **If you have an FA and investment assets, have your advisor put 5% stops on all stock & ETF positions.** If needed, you can adjust this percentage amount [from 5% to ?]. But it will help you manage risk on your stock and ETF investments.

5. **Have your advisor update your asset allocation monthly or quarterly. Have your advisor calculate the Sharpe ratio on each of your investment portfolios.** Ask this question each time your review your investments: are you being compensated with adequate returns for the risk you take in your investments?

6. **Have discussions with your advisor when you meet monthly or quarterly to discuss performance** and address any conflicts of interest you see between you, your advisor, and their advisory firm.

7. **When you look at investments, ask yourself the following questions:** a. is the risk of this investment appropriate for my portfolio? b. can I afford to lose this money if the risk is high? c. what is the probability of losing money on this investment? d. bottom line, is the reward appropriate to the risk?

Suggested reading:

1. **Handbook of Fixed income Investments,** Ninth Edition, Frank Fabozzi. Bonds are probably the least understood part of investing, for its diversity and uniqueness. I know of few experts in bonds.

2. **The Psychology of Money, Morgan Housel.**

The next chapter, chapter two, is all about how you the investor, fit into the mix of investments firms and their advisors.

Chapter Two

WHERE YOU FIT: BETWEEN FIRMS AND THEIR ADVISORS

The world of investments has many firms with financial advisors. Some are purely investment firms, others are insurance companies that own investment companies. Yet more are investment companies with insurance subsidiaries, and there are trust and fiduciary companies, all of which offer financial advisors and investments. While not all investment firms have insurance subsidiaries, most do. And many large insurers own investment companies.

The five large investment advisory firms have over **$1 trillion** each in assets under management [AUM]. They are:

1. BlackRock, with $10.08 traillion[5]

2. Vanguard, with $7.6 trillion. [6]

3. Fidelity Investments, $4.5 trillion.[7]

4. State Street Global Advisors, $4.126 trillion.[8]

---

[5] Google search, February 5th, 2024, https://s24.q4cdn.com/856567660/files/doc_financials/2023/Q4/BLK-4Q23-Earnings-Release.pdf
[6] Google search, February 5th, 2024, as of March 2023.
[7] Google search, February 5th, 2024, data as of August. 1, 2023.
[8] Google search, February 5th, 2024, State Street website, https://investors.statestreet.com/files/doc_financials/2023/q4/STT-4Q23-Earnings-Press-Release-vFinal.pdf

5. J. P. Morgan Asset Management [9]

Just because they are large does not mean they are the best. But certainly, they will have well-trained staff. I would look for a firm with at least $100 billion in assets and look for an advisor with experience who is well-trained and has the skills you need.

The top underwriting firms in the US with financial advisors are:

1. Merrill Lynch Private Wealth Management
2. UBS Wealth Advisors/Wealth Management
3. Morgan Stanley Private Wealth Management
4. Goldman Sachs Wealth Management
5. Wells Fargo Wealth Management[10]

Most of the top 100 private wealth management companies work with these top five firms, which have the most investment and insurance products.

As a firm and its professional staff, no offense, Charles Schwab has assets but I do not see they have the highest quality research, training programs for advisors, or skills to be top financial advisors. Same with Ameriprise. I have always considered these firms lower tier, and their quality, personnel, and training reflect that. I may be biased, but I worked for and trained with Merrill Lynch. Their training and skills, and

---

[9] Investopedia website, search dated 2/4/24, for top firms with over $1 trillion in assets, https://www.investopedia.com/articles/professionals/080615/5-biggest-financial-advisory-firms-us.asp#:~:text=Key%20Takeaways,assets%20under%20management%20(AUM).Also, article JP AUM, as of December 23, 2023, https://www.linkedin.com/posts/michael-c-b9846bb2_jp-morgan-reports-496-billion-profit-for-activity-7152528053166870528-SEy4

[10] Investopedia website, top-ranked US underwriting firms with financial advisors, offering full service. https://www.investopedia.com/articles/professionals/080615/5-biggest-financial-advisory-firms-us.asp#:~:text=The%20following%20five%20financial%20advisory,and%20J.P.%20Morgan%20Asset%20Management.

breadth of expertise and products was unrivaled. Very few firms rival them.

Forbes also has a list of top wealth management advisors; I would check this out either from a subscription or your local library. Barron's also has a list of top wealth management advisory firms.

There are plenty of firms and an abundance of financial advisors. You will have to do some due diligence to find the right firm and advisor. My biggest competition for business at Merrill Lynch was usually competing with another Merrill advisor.

How to Find a Financial Advisor [or hire a new one]:

Consider finding a firm near you and someone you know who is an advisor. You can find the top firms in your area by looking at your local business journal, which most likely rates the financial advisory firms in your city and/or state. If you need a subscription to your local business journal, research them at your local library. If you have an advisor, I will give you recommendations at the end of this chapter, to help you function better with them, to gain wealth and more positive results.

Further, get financial statements on the firms that interest you. If they are private, you will have to show interest in doing business with them for them to release their financials to you. Please make sure the financial statements of the advisory firm are audited and that the auditor says the statements fairly represent their financial standing. If the auditor's opinion is qualified, then find another firm. A qualified financial opinion means that the firm may not be a going concern, that the auditor, a CPA firm, has doubts about its ability to continue to exist.

Look at the income statement for your potential firm: where do their revenues come from in terms of products? Most will have sales of investment and insurance products. Merrill Lynch was an underwriter also, so Merrill's advisors were notified when Merrill Lynch completed an underwriting, either of an Initial Public Offering, stock or bond underwriting, or an alternative investment.

If you deal with a firm like Merrill Lynch, know that they are making fees as an underwriter and selling these products. It broadens the range of investments you can participate in, yet some of these products they underwrite are highly risky and may not be appropriate to your risk tolerance or portfolio. Advisors who sell these products get high sales commissions for these products. Beware of products with high sales commissions. Some are worth it, many are not. Just because your firm underwrote the investment [got fees for that], does not mean it is a good investment for you.

When your advisor sells you a high-commission product, there may be conflicts of interest. Merrill Lynch makes fees when underwriting and a Merrill Lynch advisor may make a high commission when selling that product.

Beware if the product being sold, such as an alternative investment, is being offered to you if you have a moderate risk tolerance, middle of the road, concerning risk. This product only fits your portfolio if you are a growth or aggressive investor.

As for advisors, check out their investment records with clients, and seek references. Ask for a letter of good standing from their branch manager. That will help you avoid hiring an advisor who is not in good standing with the firm and may be fired for failing to meet the company's sales quota. Know that each firm has sales goals for its advisors. New advisors going through training programs may have aggressive sales goals to filter out who is best at achieving the firm's goals.

To be clear, the firm you hire will exercise control over your advisor. They will have to have good rapport with compliance and the branch manager and have few complaints against them. It would be wise to ask for the advisor's complaint file over the last 3-5 years.

The advisor's complaint file will tell you if the advisor is in hot water over his performance with clients. Mistakes happen, but an abundance of errors or conflicts reflect that the advisor needs to meet their client's performance goals, not merely the firm's sales goals. **There is the conflict common to clients:** your advisor has to meet sales goals, and that pressure may press them to offer products or services not appropriate for you.

When interviewing an advisor, go to their office and get a feel for the place. Is it friendly? Does it feel like their branch manager strongly influences or controls people? Each office will have a feel. Is your potential advisor relaxed or uptight? Do they answer all your questions in detail?

Does this advisor make promises that they can keep? Be careful if the advisor or his superiors try too hard to win you as a client. They should be pleasant, conversational, and professional, be well trained, and be able to answer what the firm and the advisor does best while not overworking to get your business.

Find an advisor with the skills you need. If you primarily need an investment advisor who will give you asset allocation for your investments, manage risk, and monitor performance, focus on that. If you are new to saving and investments, focus on the insurance aspects, planning factors, defining goals and how long it takes to reach them, continue saving, and later focus on investments.

It depends on your financial plan, how long you have been saving for investments and financial goals, the income and assets you have to work with, and your desired level of risk, which influences who or which advisor is best for you now. **If you have less than $100,000 in liquid assets**, you should focus first on risk management: making sure you handle the risks that would be catastrophic to your long term wealth, such as health, life, property and liability insurance. You can save in your company's 401K plan, and when you have $100,000 to $250,000, then you are attractive as an investment client. Until then, keep saving and investing with your company's 401K plan, or an IRA if your company does not have a 401K plan.

Most financial advisory firms have research, and some research is better than others. You might find out what the area of specialty is for that firm: no one firm is best in all the areas of investment. Do they specialize in small-capitalization stocks? In medium or large-capitalization stocks? In International Stocks? In Municipal Bonds? In Emerging Markets? In Alternative investments? In growth stocks?

Know that fiduciary and trust companies will likely be more conservative, some merely capital preservation companies. Many are sleepy. lag with research and serices, and do not offer the same level of products or services as the top-tier firms.

If you wish to have cutting-edge research and stock investments, look elsewhere than Trust and Fiduciary companies. There may be exceptions, and some sleepier trust companies have woken up and produced meaningful research. Good research is an excellent benefit to the firm you choose. I had Merrill Lynch research on small, medium, and large-cap stocks and emerging markets, along with value and growth analysis within small-mid- and large-capitalization stocks, plusi Economic, Investment, and specific asset class reports, along with recommended asset allocations, company reports, and bond research. It vastly improved my job performance and gave me more time to spend with clients & manage their investments. Few firms offers all of these products and services to their advisors. And remember, no advisor is an expert in everything you need. Does this firm have the research for investments in the area most important to you, such as Large cap stocks, mid-cap growth, and corporate bonds? **Bottom line: You want your advisor to have good research.**

Talk about fees with the firm. Do they have a fee schedule? I found that the best, most fairest way to determine investment expenses for a client was to place client assets in an asset management account, and we agreed on the fee, negotiated between my client and me. We set these fees between 1% and 2.0 %, depending on the amount of the assets. Fee-based investing works well for clients with $100,000 or more in assets. Included in the fees, were any stock trades I would make, buying either a stock or an ETF, any bonds that I would buy, and any cash management product that I would buy. When I bought ETF's, I held most of them for the long-term, and clients gained by the lower cost structure of the investment.

This asset management account reflected all the fees charged to my client. So, I would not buy a mutual fund within this account, as that would raise costs. I was an MBA, CFP, and CFA, so I read Merrill Lynch's research and then designed portfolios from this research. Reading research to create portfolios is time-consuming, but I also got superior returns above the market for all of my career. When downturns occurred, I quickly raised cash and bond levels and got out of stocks. I beat the market every year that I worked as an investment advisor, for twelve years.

Crucial issues I experienced as a Financial Advisor:

1. **I inherited some accounts from Merrill Lynch by being a new advisor.** I generally found these accounts to have been abandoned and not managed by the prior advisor. When I called clients, most were glad to hear from me. Some rejected the advice and thought they knew better than I did or wanted to be the portfolio manager. I learned to manage where clients wanted me to: on some accounts, I fired the client, as I realized I could not function well if clients did not allow me to perform my job, which was to analyze

investments and make investment recommendations. Your take-away: make sure you get at least quarterly investment recommen-dations and reviews if you have $100,000 or more in investment assets and monthly investment reviews and advice if you have $250,000 or more in investments.

2. **I learned that advisors were constantly coming and going.** Some went to new firms for more pay, and some advisors got fired for non-performance. Merrill Lynch scared the daylights out of me daily, as we were always going to get trained, present ourselves, to tell Merrill trainers about products. This field is only for some. It makes me ask the question: how does your advisor handle stress? How many hours do they work per week? Do they have plenty of investment assets, so they are not in danger of being fired? Are they in good standing with their firm?

3. **I learned that it is better to have happy clients and charge them a reasonable fee** than to make money from a few high-commis-sion product sales and possibly lose these investors as clients. I took a long-term perspective instead of a short-term one.

4. **I learned that most firms, including Merrill Lynch, want finan-cial advisors who gather assets**, work primarily as relationship managers with clients, and invest in Merrill Lynch products. That is unethical unless Merrill has the best products in all categories, which they do not. It is not ethical because financial advisors are meant to be independent. Despite compliance departments, only some firms care about advisors' independence. Most say their ad-visors are independent: I would argue that most advisors are not. Advisory firms want the fees from your investing. It is up to you to be sure that your advisor acts independently. Frankly, no one at the firm that employs your advisor will help you accomplish that.

5. **I was an MBA & CFA, the same qualifications that most portfolio managers held**. Mother Merrill was not pleased that I wanted to manage the retirement assets of my clients. They were more concerned with making money off their products than me being independent and managing money for my clients. It was very disappointing that they did not want advisors managing money. I found it challenging to be a glorified customer relationship manager. Merrill Lynch wanted me to gather more assets and let Merrill make more money in fees. If you don't please mother Merrill, you can substantially shorten your career at the firm.

6. **After working at Merrill Lynch, I worked at a Houston branch of Guardian Life Insurance company.** I gained more knowledge and familiarity with insurance products, such as life, disability, and long-term care insurance, and superior knowledge of financial planning. My disappointment there was that Guardian wanted you to sell insurance products. Guardian forced you to do a great deal of financial planning, to sell insurance products, not investments. Guardian purposely limited the number of products so that investment choices were much less than Merrill Lynch, and stock trades had to have manual one-page forms, hand-written, for each transaction. I quickly learned that having an insurance and planning background was great, but not at the cost of my client's investment choices. I was substantially limited in investing [primarily with high-fee mutual funds] having limited products and way too much compliance, limiting my freedom to make choices for my investment clients. I decided later, after gaining more training, to move to another firm.

7. **My third and last investment advisory firm was Woodbury**. I found them to have excellent product choices and give their advisors freedom among insurance and investment products. It was definitely a firm for more experienced advisors who had built their

clientele and were ready to invest and provide insurance products as needed. I appreciated having the freedom to offer my clients what they needed and do as much or as little financial planning as my clients needed or as I saw fit. Financial planning is great. Every financial plan has to be updated, and some are destroyed by the actions of your client.

8. **Merrill Lynch and Woodbury provided the best investment platforms I experienced as a Financial Advisor**. In both places, there were significant downturns in equity markets, especially in 2001 and 2008. Both firms had excellent research, and out of both downturns, I was aggressive with investing, usually 70% equities even for moderate risk tolerance investors and 80% equities for growth investors. Both times, my clients experienced returns of over 100% in the next two years following those equity declines. I had not lost the money at Merrill as I was training and building my business after equity markets had declined. At Woodbury, I had 5% stops on all equity investments, and my retirement clients needed more equity investments. Nor did I lose money for clients at Guardian insurance.

9. **The significance of my investing after downturns is that it usually only took one fiscal quarter to get clients back their money** [which was lost by another advisor]. It takes a substantially extended period to get back your money when you have lost 20%, 30%, or more. In investing, it is best to minimize losses and preserve your gains. It takes a hands on advisor to protect your money in downturns, and gain as much as possible, per your risk tolerance, when equity and bond markets are rising.

10. **Many retirement plans have been destroyed during market downturns**, with overly aggressive asset allocations, and with financial advisors who are too busy looking for clients rather than

managing your money. And if the advisor has you primarily invested in the firm's products, that may please his bosses at the firm but may not be appropriate for you. Botttom line: you must hold your advisor accountable for the investment performance of your investments. Most are too busy chasing and gathering assets to monitor your investments. And no one at the firm, including their compliance department, will make sure that your assets are well managed. You have to be the one to keep your advisor accountable for their investment performance.

Here are suggestions of questions that you ask your potential or current advisors when you interview them:

1. Why did you choose this firm to build your career as a financial advisor? How long have you been in business?

2. What are the specialty skills of your firm?

3. What was your primary area of training within the firm?

4. How would you describe the quality of your firm's investment research in both stocks and bonds and alternative investments?

5. Whose research do you rely on to make investment choices and determine asset allocations for your clients?

6. How do you manage investment risk?

7. How do you quantify risk in investment portfolios?

8. How much $$$ do you manage in terms of Investments?

9. Do you primarily function as a portfolio manager, or do you primarily work as client service and let your firm invest the assets in their funds? How much of your client's investment assets are managed by your firm or you?

10. Do you have a team? How many members are on your team? What does each person do?

11. How often would you meet with us to review our investment portfolio performance?

12. Do you create financial plans for all of your clients? [Such as plan to meet your goals: retirement, donating to charities or children, buying or selling a business, etc.]

There may be conflicts between your financial goals, your firm, and your advisor.

What are some of the conflicts between advisors and their clients?

1. **Investment firms, insurance companies, and advisors all have goals.** Be aware that Advisory firm goals and advisor quotas may conflict with your goals. If an advisor makes a recommendation that is hard to comprehend or does not make sense, ask: What are your fees on this investment? Ask them to clarify how this investment helps you achieve your financial goals. What are my risks of losing money on this investment? Do the returns earned compensate me for all this risk I am taking on this investment? Ask how your advisor is quantifying risk and return. If you are unsatisfied, it may be time to hire another advisor. Here the issue is the product being offered.

2. **You may have multiple advisors.** Each wants to look at all your portfolios and is trying to accumulate all your assets. You will have to decide who is performing and who is being accountable, and then decide if you should move all your investment assets to one or two advisors or maintain multiple advisors. It depends on you: your life is more complex with multiple advisors, but it may be

worth it if each is an expert in what they do and they are accountable & perform.

3. **Be sure that your advisor is reviewing your assets, participating in gains, and not losing money.** I suggest monthly or quarterly portfolio reviews. Check your net rate of return after expenses, and compare it to returns on the Standard & Poor's 500 index or whatever is the most appropriate benchmark for your portfolio. If your advisor is not willing to do this, hire another advisor who is ready to be accountable.

My goal is to help you get the right advisory firm, with the right products for you, with the right advisor who will diligently oversee your money, give you timely advice, carefully watch the investment performance, and then make changes to your investments as needed, frequent conversations and meetings about your investments and their performance.

Have investment rules established with your Advisor regarding when to buy stocks and ETFs and when to sell.

For example, a potential buy rule for an individual stock or ETF could be: P/E ratio less than S&P 500, Revenue and Profit growth more significant than the S&P 500 average, in an industry/sector with positive growth expectations, say 10% per year, meaning it is a timely purchase, in the early stages of growth for the year [meaning the performance is yet to come, not already passed].

A potential sell rule for equities could be: Sell when the overall equity market, such as the S&P 500, is down 3% or more in a day, or 5% in a week, when the industry or sector growth deteriorates, or when profits or profit estimates are down 10% or more for the specific equity or ETF, for the current year. This all requires careful monitoring. That is where most advisors fail. They do not have systems in place to monitor this for all their investment clients.

Additionally, if the $VIX [volatility index] spikes by 20% or more in one day; this could trigger getting out of equity positions until the VIX declines to more normal levels [defined in the sell rule].

You can also develop a **bond sell rule** with your Advisor and a bond expert in your firm. Before rates rise, I suggest you create this rule to address interest rate risk in your portfolio. Also, you should address the deterioration in the investment rating of the bonds, do your best to have this rule before that occurs, and have research on your bonds to inform you when changes should be made in your bond portfolio.

In my experience, most investment clients with $1 million to $10 million in investment assets are moderate investors, leading to a more conservative stop if you place stops [sell orders] on your equity positions.

In the next chapter, Chapter Three, we will discuss Investment products in more detail.

Chapter Three

ECONOMICS, CHALLENGES, & ITS IMPACT ON INVESTING

This chapter explains the influence of the US economy and its impact on investing, and investment reports, which discuss the US economy, sectors, and company performance, and makes recommendations on what to buy. The goal here is to integrate investment knowledge which is first rooted in economics and economic data. So we will review an investment report discussing the US economy, and then make application to its impact on investments and investing.

US Economic Outlook

The US economy's growth has faced several headwinds from 2020-2022 by Covid, corporate workers working at home and working fewer hours, lower productivity, inflation, the Federal Reserve substantially raising interest rates, along with the war in Ukraine. Despite these challenges, the US industrial production index recovered from a low of 84 in October 2022 to 103 by February 2022. In 2023, retail sales grew 4.9% for the year [excluding auto and gasoline sales], and personal income rose 4.2% and personal savings rose to 4.5%.[11] Consumer spending was slow in the first two quarters of 2023, and although personal savings

---

[11] Per Commerce department website, dated February 6, 2024. https://www.commerce.gov/news/blog/2024/01/numbers-us-economy-grows-faster-expected-year-and-final-quarter-2023#:~:text=For%20the%20full%20year%2C%20retail,to%204.5%20percent%20in%202023.

increased, so did household debt and delinquencies, with. household debt rising to $17.5 trillion,[12] from $16.38 trillion in 2022[13], a rise of 6.8%.

Inflation was significant in 2022 and 2023 for both businesses & consumers, primarily due to energy and higher household food costs. The Consumer price index was up 9.1% in 2022 through June. In late 2022, consumer prices decreased with lower gas and food prices, and continued a downward trend for 2023. The CPI rose 3.4% for 2023.[14]

The US federal government continues to run $1 trillion deficits, causing the Federal government to borrow money. Inflation came from lower US oil drilling and production, higher energy costs, Avian flu connected to egg production, and higher gasoline demand. In 2023, the US federal deficit was $1.7 trillion.[15]

Interest rates continue to rise, as the Federal Reserve made seven rate increases to the Fed Funds rate in 2022, raising interest rates by 2.25%, and in 2023, rate increases of 1.00%. The Federal Reserve is on a mission to tame inflation, and the effects of this are increased borrowing costs for businesses and consumers. The Federal Funds rate increased

---

[12] Per February 6th search, website https://www.aa.com.tr/en/americas/us-household-debt-climbs-to-175t-in-4q-of-2023-fed/3129651#:~:text=US%20house-hold%20debt%20climbs%20to%20%2417.5T%20in%204Q%20of%202023%3A%2oFed

[13] USA Today website, search dated February 6, 2024, https://www.usato-day.com/money/blueprint/debt/average-american-debt-statistics/#:~:text=To-tal%20consumer%20debt%20balances%20in-creased,4.15%25%20over%20the%20past%20year.

[14] CNBC website, Google search dated February 6th, 2024, https://www.cnbc.com/2024/01/11/cpi-inflation-report-december-2023-consumer-prices-rose-0point3percent-in-december-higher-than-expected-pushing-the-annual-rate-to-3point4percent.html#:~:text=The%20consumer%20price%20index%20in-creased%200.3%25%20for%20the%20month%2C%20higher,%2Dyear%20read-ing%20of%203.2%25.

[15] Google search dated February 7, 2024, website of the Bipartisan Policy Center, https://bipartisanpolicy.org/report/deficit-tracker/#:~:text=Fis-cal%20Year%202023%20in%20Review,%25)%20year%2Dover%2Dyear.

nearly 5%, raising interest rates significantly for lines of credit, home mortgages, and home equity loans. In total the Federal Reserve raised rates seven times in 2022 totaling 4.25%, and four times in 2023, for a total of 1%. The rise in rates has made home ownership less affordable, and this accounts for much of the rise in delinquencies on home mortgages.

Silicon Valley Bank went bankrupt in 2023, primarily due to losses on its bond portfolio. Overall, the US banking system investment portfolios are full of losses on their bond portfolios, from owning with maturities greater than 20 years, as interest rates rise, long bond values go down.

US Asset Class Performance

US equity markets bottomed out in October 2022. Comparing assets classes as of February 21, 2023, the three best-performing asset classes so far in 2023 are: the Vanguard Total Stock Market Index [ticker VTI], up 7.55% YTD, the Ishares 20+ year Treasury Bond Index [ticker TLT], up 2.51% YTD, Invesco's US dollar index fund [ticker UUP] is up .93% YTD and SPDR Gold Shares [ticker GLD] up .86% for 2023. The largest equity gainers in 2023 were tech stocks, [the Magnificent Seven, Nvidia, Alphabet, Amazon, Apple, Microsoft, Tesla, and Meta] with large cap stocks up 25%,

US equities vs. International equities

Comparing US equities to International equities, The Vanguard Total International Stock Index ETF [ticker VTI] was up 26% in 2023YTD, while the Vanguard Developed Markets index [ticker VEA] was up 17.9%[16], while the emerging markets index [ticker VWO] lagged the US and developed international stocks.

---

[16] Capital Spectator website, newsletter, on their website, from Google search, dated February 6th, 2024, https://www.capitalspectator.com/major-asset-classes-december-2023-performance-review/

The S&P 500 earned 25% in the US in 2023 [as of 2/21/23], while the Dow Jones Industrial average was up 14% for 2023.[17] The S&P Midcap 400 was up 16.4% for the year, while the S&P 600 Small cap index was up 16.1%.[18] So, large caps were up more than Midcaps, and Midcaps are up more than small cap stocks, reflected in the S&P 500. All of these US indexes and market caps are beating international stocks.

Sector Performance

The three leading sectors, all with positive returns, were Technology, Communication Services, and Consumer Cyclical/Discretionary.

Technology

In a breakthrough year, the promise of AI's potential catapulted the tech sector to 56% returns.

Chipmaker Nvidia skyrocketed 239% as demand for AI chips accelerated. Apple and Microsoft each had banner years after a dismal 2022. Overall, big tech stocks were responsible for a large share of the S&P 500's gains.

In fact, the "Magnificent Seven"—made up of Nvidia, Apple, Microsoft, Alphabet, Amazon, Tesla, and Meta—drove an estimated 75% of the market's returns and together, they cover about 30% of its total value.

Communication Services

As the second-best sector, communication services rallied 54% in 2023. From media and internet companies to telecom and broadband service

---

[17] Google search dated February 6, 2024, Nasdaq website, https://www.nasdaq.com/articles/5-biggest-winners-5-biggest-losers-from-dow-jones-industrial-average-in-2023#:~:text=Why%20It%27s%20Important%3A%20After%20being,which%20saw%20an%208.5%25%20decline.

[18] Google search, dated February 6th, 2024, Wilbanks, Smith, and Thomas website, https://www.wstam.com/news/market-updates/december-2023-global-equity-markets-review/

providers, the sector covers a diverse range of companies—many that may stand to benefit from generative AI.

With 194% gains, Meta was a top performer as advertising revenue improved. At the same time, Netflix (+65%), Alphabet (+59%), and video game publisher Take-Two Interactive (+55%) each saw strong momentum.

Consumer Cyclical/Discretionary

In one of the best years on record, the S&P 500 consumer discretionary sector witnessed over 41% returns. Amazon, Home Depot, and Tesla fall within this sector and each saw at least double-digit returns supported by solid retail sales. Tesla is projected to see record deliveries in 2023.

Cruise-line operator Royal Caribbean was a leading company, with over 162% returns for the year. Record travel demand drove strong performance across both Royal Caribbean and Carnival.

The poorest-performing sectors for 2023 were defensive sectors, including Utilities, Energy, and Consumer Staples.

Utilities

With -10% returns, utilities declined the most as high interest rates weighed on borrowing costs in the capital-intensive sector. Not only that, utilities became less attractive as 10-year Treasury yields were higher than utilities dividend yields in 2023—a first in over a decade. In this way, investors looking for income shifted away from the sector. The good news for utilities is that interest rates are projected to fall over the next several years, according to IMF projections.

Energy

Oil prices declined 10% in 2023, and the sector also ended in the red. Despite OPEC+ production cuts aimed to boost prices, key benchmarks sank 20% from their annual peak. Devon Energy, one of the largest

American shale producers declined 22% and Chevron dropped 14% as oil production and refinery operations missed targets.

Consumer Staples/Defensive

While the consumer staples outperformed in 2022, investors had a different view on it this year. This led to a mixed bag of returns in the sector.

Known for companies that make everyday items, consumer staples covers Coca-Cola, Procter & Gamble, and Walmart. Within the sector, packaged food faced some of the worst declines amid competition from lower-priced products as consumers looked to more affordable options.[19]

Recommended Asset Allocation

Please note that I am summarizing data here and not giving specific investment advice. Note this is a disclaimer and not recommended investment advice. The goal here is to give you an indication of choosing investments in the current economic environment.

Due to the likelihood that the Federal Reserve will continue to raise interest rates to fight inflation, longer maturity bonds will likely lose money in the short term, leading to lower bond allocations with higher rates of cash and commodities.

I will be generic here to avoid giving specific investment advice, as it may be untimely for you:

1. **I would hold 20% cash for all portfolios in present conditions due to likely interest-rate increases and further equity declines.** To minimize bond losses, I would have 20% of my bond allocation primarily in

---

[19] Per Google search, Visual Capitalist website, best and worst performing sectors of 2023, YTD performance https://www.visualcapitalist.com/best-and-worst-performing-sectors-in-2023/#

1-3 year Treasury and Investment grade municipal securities. So that is the position for cash and bonds, 50%.

2. **I would hold stocks primarily in high dividend-paying stocks**, such as Vanguard High Dividend-paying stocks and ticker VYM, with a YTD return of 6.53% return as of 2/6/24, with a dividend of 3.12%. It will likely outperform other .stocks, while the market is facing severe obstacles: interest rate increases [up nearly 5% in the last year], plus inflation, plus the war in Ukraine, and that US banks are weak, and consumers are still overcoming inflation of the past several years

3. **For moderate and higher risk tolerance portfolios**, I would look for lower risk income streams, with investments in real-estate, such as timber and oil-producing properties. Also, for these portfolios, I would buy and sell options, to maximize income and lower risk and consider hedges for interest-rate risk and lower equity prices in the short term.

How I responded to economic & investment research:

My experience as an investment advisor and portfolio manager with clients was constantly communicating market conditions and having recommendations if their portfolio positions needed to be changed. I primarily managed risk with 5% stops on all equity positions, and when equity markets were falling, I went to cash and held more bonds.

I wrote an investment newsletter and shared it with clients weekly. I performed monthly portfolio reviews for investment portfolios with $250,000 or more and quarterly for investment accounts with $100,000 to $250,000. Advisors should review client accounts with $1 million or more in investments weekly. And since I had significant client assets in annuities, annuities were also reviewed monthly or quarterly, with the same guidelines.

Know that most financial advisors sell annuities but do not manage those investments. And most advisors are busy chasing more assets, as their firms require. Your investments should be reviewed according to these guidelines, but most advisors do not check their clients' investments as often as they should.

If your advisor is an asset gatherer, meaning that they do not manage your investments but allocate your investment accounts primarily to their firms or other investment products, there is no reason for them not to review your accounts. And if they are a portfolio manager, there is all the more reason for them to check your accounts, as they are responsible for the results. In truth, your advisor is accountable for the results regardless.

Most advisors blame the fund managers or the economy for poor performance, but your advisor should be offering solutions and products, even in market downturns. Your advisor should change your asset allocation, especially when equity markets are going down. If your advisor is not updating you on market conditions, reviewing your accounts, or meeting with you to suggest new investments or change what you have, they are not doing their job. Their job is first to manage your investments responsibly and secondarily to seek more assets. If they are not good stewards of what they have, why should they be given more?

Due to current interest-rate risk, moving from bonds to higher cash positions is better. And if your advisor can, and your firm allows it, use some risk management products, such as options or futures, as hedges on interest rate risk and equity declines.

Warning: there may be a conflict with your firm in using risk-management products, such as shorts and hedges, in your investment accounts. That is old thinking. Your compliance department may say that risk-management tools are inappropriate for your account. Know that Compliance is wrong., It would be best to have an advisor that uses risk-management products and a firm that allows you to use them. If your advisor or firm does not approve of you using risk management products, such as ETF shorts [like pro shares SH] and hedges, you should fire your advisor and firm and find another.

Also, your advisor's firm may not allow its advisors to write newsletters and share them with clients. Newsletters are a compliance issue, where the firm's compliance department reviews this information. They do this primarily to limit their liability more than they care that the advisor can get critical information to their clients. They may only allow the advisor to email the firm's investment research, which is fine, only if that research offers analysis & updates on the US economy, US and international investment climate, specific recommendations on asset allocation, and specific investments in equities and bonds.

Additional warning: some advisory firms will not allow you the freedom to invest in alternative investments, such as real estate, timber, or oil-producing properties. Such investments help your advisor manage risk or add income streams when equity markets fall. When added to a portfolio, they help reduce risk and provide income. Imagine how important this is when you are taking distributions from your retirement investments and equity markets are decreasing.

You must know what investment products are allowed for alternative investments, shorts, and hedges. If alternative investments are not permitted at your firm, find one that does. The advisory firms that do not allow these products are more worried about their risks, such as losing you as a client, than preserving your money. If your current firm or advisory does not offer alternative investments and risk management products, find a new advisory firm and a new advisor.

Now that we have given you a sample of a good investment report, discussing the US economy, and US stock performance compared to international stocks, and offered the best performing US sectors and the lagging US sectors, we will now discuss what makes a good investment report.

What makes a good investment report:

1. **Outlining what is driving current economic conditions, what sectors are performing and which are not**, dramatically improves portfolio choices. Knowing what interest rates are doing is also beneficial. What the Federal Reserve is doing with rates helps you see if you need to be more careful with bond investments, say, when interest rates are rising [and equity markets tend to lag] versus when the Federal Reserve cuts interest rates [and markets tend to rise, more than normal]. Also, equities & ETFs respond in the opposite direction of interest rate moves. If the Federal Reserve is raising rates, stocks usually go down: if the Federal Reserve is cutting interest rates, stocks typically respond very positively to those changes. So, the direction of interest rates gives the advisor relevant information about allocations to bonds and equities.

2. **Then knowing what is performing best:** international or US stocks? Small-cap, mid-cap, or large-cap? Value or growth? All help to allocate $$$ to investments.

3. **It always helps clients to know how each portfolio performed, YTD and relative to the market.** Each investment portfolio needs a benchmark return that measures your portfolio return against this benchmark. You need to have a benchmark for each investment portfolio and an advisor willing to account for their performance.

Why Economic analysis of markets is essential:

Interest rate increases or decreases likely tell you equity market direction. Interest rate rises usually lead to lower stock prices, and interest rate cuts typically lead to advancing and growing equity markets. Your advisor should increase your equity allocation if equity markets are strong and rising.

If you are fighting interest rate increases, you have to be careful with bonds as they tend to lose money when interest rates rise, and you may need to decrease your investment portfolio allocation to bonds. And you need to increase the use of risk-management products. It is best to use stops on your investment portfolio, primarily lowering these stops to 3%, to minimize investment losses.

Additionally, higher inflation means less consumer spending. Some businesses like Home Depot and Lowe's, such as Consumer discretionary stocks, will find the economic environment much more challenging to make money. Consumers will spend more on food and gas in this tighter money environment and less on discretionary projects, such as upgrading their homes.

Other indicators, such as the US manufacturing index, indicate where the US is in the business cycle, which usually lasts three to four years and has early middle and late effects which favor specific sectors.

For example, sectors that do well in the early stages of a new business cycle are the construction and manufacturing sectors rise, and retail sectors start to increase earnings. In the middle of a rising business cycle, energy, technology, and information technology are growing. Near the end of a business cycle, sectors that do well are consumer staples [such as food, electricity, and gasoline] do well, along with prescription drugs.

As an advisor, I was always looking at what was performing well. I found that, at times, it was too late to invest in some sectors, as the money had already been made and was being invested elsewhere. I always asked myself: should I take gains and move to new positions that are growing faster? It is always good for an advisor to know which sectors are performing, which are on the rise, and which are falling.

The US economy versus the World Economy

Business cycles play out all over the world. Emerging markets, such as China and Brazil, grow fast than most developed markets, such as the US and western Europe. Therefore, it helps to know internationally which economies are growing, which are in recession, and which have next to zero growth. Equities usually do better in faster-growing economies.

Challenges to investing: inflation, US federal debt, & taxes

One currently underrated issue for investing is inflation. What happens to your financial plan if inflation exceeds most investment returns in bonds and equities? It means that you are losing money, and getting back inflated dollars. This is not a recipe for success. Equities and real estate are usually used in financial and investment strategies, within retirement accounts for example, to beat inflation, and create real gains. Excessive Inflation can ruin a retirement plan.

Know that the US government's reported rates of inflation are overly low. They say inflation was, for example, 3% when it was likely 7% to 10%, in the past several years, especially 2020-2024. Why do they do that? Well, governments want to say they are doing a good job. No US president likes to say he is doing a terrible job with the economy. So, this is a common lie to cover printed money and overspending.

Think about how destructive inflation is to your portfolio: if your portfolio makes 10% this year, but inflation is 8%, you only gained 2%, which is not much of a gain. I say this because the US has printed so much money in the last few years, from 2020 [from $4 trillion dollars in existence in 2020 to $20 trillion dollars today.[20]] Regardless of who is President, inflation will be higher than you or I planned, going forward.

---

[20] Google search dated February 6th, 2024, website
https://techstartups.com/2021/12/18/80-us-dollars-existence-printed-january-2020-october-2021/

Fighting the adverse effects of inflation requires more risk management tools in your investment portfolio to hedge interest rates in your bond portfolios and inflation risks in your bond and equity portfolios. Your advisor needs to address these risks more profoundly than ever. Will they use options or futures to hedge your interest rate risk? Does your financial advisor or firm have the skills and experience to do this? Will your advisory firm allow you to do this? The **bottom line** is that only some firms have the products, skills, and structures to manage these investment risks and offer them to their private wealth clients. **Make sure** that you have such a firm and such an advisor.

A primary cause of inflation in the United States is the dramatic increase in debt since 2000. In September 2000, the US federal debt was $5.7 trillion. Ten years later, by September 2010, this exact debt figure was $13.7 trillion. Currently, the US federal debt [February 3, 2024] is $34.155 trillion.

The US Federal Government has used the historically low borrowing rates of the past ten years to fund crushing amounts of debt, meaning borrowing long-term at 2-3%, which in 2023 these rates climbed to 5-6%. The US federal debt has increased 249% (using simple math) in the last 12 years and over 599% during the previous 22 years (again, simple math). Borrowing this much money is not sustainable, no matter how low-interest rates are. **How long can you borrow more than your yearly income?** That is what the US has been doing for some time now. And the investors who bought 2-3% long-bonds, and saw interest rates double and triple in 2023 lost their shirts. That is what sunk Silicon Valley Bank.

Why is US government [treasury] borrowing unsustainable? Other nations and their investors will not continue to buy US debt. The US can only sustainably borrow up to its income yearly. Eventually, the US debt would crowd out all other long-term bond investments. Until the US is declared bankrupt for its debt, when it can no longer pay with historically higher interest rates, it will likely have continuously higher inflation and taxes. Right now, the US government is having budgeting problems: it can no longer pay for Social Security and Medicare and pay for defense without cutting one or the other. Cuts to the US budget are needed: I would not want social security or medicare benefits cut. These changes are coming, and most investors must prepare for them. Governments threatened by bankruptcy could nationalize the assets of companies & investors [taking your investment assets or taxing them to death, say with 50% or more tax]. That is a real risk to US investors based on the US national debt. Most financial advisors do not discuss this threat to your retirement plans and investment assets.

The US federal government may be required to balance its budget by the financial market's more austere conditions, such as inflation, taxes, possible bankruptcy, and potentially a new currency. These current patterns of debt and borrowing and inflation cannot continue for long. These conditions will affect all US investors and could plunge the US economy into a depression for a decade or more. That would severely damage every US citizen's finances, & especially stock and bond portfolios. These issues of inflation, debt, and taxes will significantly influence investing and your investment values for the next twenty-five years. How will they impact your portfolio? Do you have an advisor that can answer this question?

An extremely critical issue in investing is the tax structure of your investment vehicles. Most clients accumulate money in IRAs, which are taxable when you take cash out. Let's say you earn $3 million in your IRA: and you assume that you will have 35% taxes. What happens if income taxes are 50% or more? Well, it blows up your plan, because it effectively cuts your savings into half [you lose $450,000 of money that would have been distributed to you]. No advisor in existence can predict what future tax rates will be. Estimating future income tax rates is like shooting darts: you rarely hit the bullseye, and mostly you guess. Most advisors have guessed that taxes during retirement will be low [again, a substantial risk to blowing up a retirement plan]. I do not believe that taxes on retirement assets will be low.

The federal government has printed a significant amount of money in the US due to deficits, COVID, and poor economic performance. The national debt is $34.155 trillion [now, February 2, 2024] more than the US GDP for 2023, which was $27.36 trillion.

If you understand what I have said about inflation, taxes, & debt, you will likely face much higher taxes than in the past. That makes tax-free investing worth more, or in taxable now structures [a taxable investment account], where the taxes have been or are paid currently, instead of in future tax scenarios like IRAs. A tax efficient IRA is a ROTH IRA: you don't get deductions when you invest in one, but when you take money out, you get credit for your contributions. Even a taxable investment account is superior to a regular IRA when you take distributions, as you have a basis for your assistance.

In my humble opinion, most investment clients do not value investing in ROTH IRAs, or even in tax-free insurance structures, such as life insurance, to minimize taxes. Most clients are trying to gain as much wealth as they can within taxable structures, and they will have to pay whatever income tax rates are in the future. I do not support this strategy.

Closing thoughts

1. **Investment reports are great for stock choices when you have a lot of data,** such as when equity investments have been on a solid uptrend for years. When equities switch directions, trending down, it takes time to have fundamental data that explains what is happening in the US Economy, sectors, etc. At this point, I rely more on technical analysis and charts describing what is happening in equity markets. At the same time, I wait for fundamental data to

verify economic indicators and specific information on companies and stocks that my clients own. **Most advisors do not move fast enough to sell stocks and move out of equities at these times.**

2. **Also, during these significant turns n the equity market's direction**, I rely on my 5% stops to take gains and minimize losses from an uptrend to a downtrend. From experience, most advisors watch their clients' equity positions fall, as most do not have the expertise to sell equities or avoid client losses. If a client takes distributions on a $1 million portfolio, losing 20% or $200,000 can easily take 2 or 3 years of distributions from their investments. So, closely managing risk always stays in style with these clients.

3. **For example, Home Depot fell 7% during the week of February 21-24th, 2023.** [Monday was President's day, so no trading]. Home Depot fell 7%, mostly in one day, due to lower expectations of earnings. Consumer discretionary funds are much lower due to inflation and thus will spend less money on home improvements. That was a massive move for one week, and most of this move came in one day. That is a quick adjustment for owners of this stock. I would have adjusted my stops during this period of higher volatility to 3% on stocks in this sector, consumer discretionary, to minimize losses. This is an example of adjusting to market volatility.

4. **You should use risk management products using a volatility index**, such as the ticker $VIX. In 2022, this index spiked above 30 six times, which would be the best time to use a short or a hedge. You and your advisor could establish rules about when to use risk management products, such as an equity short, when the volatility index spikes. Discuss with your advisor about using risk management products, such as shorts and hedges. Ask them to develop a risk management strategy for you. For example, when the $VIX

spikes 20% of more in a week, buy risk-management products, specially, TBD.

5. **In equity investments, fundamental data (such as economic reports and reports on sectors) is most useful for long-term investing when equity markets to increase**. When equity markets move down, the short-term technical data from charts work best to know what is happening and what is happening with 50-day and 200-day moving averages. So, technical charts are key when equity markets change direction because advisors and their investors wait for fundamental data to confirm what is happening.

6. **Unless your advisor regularly reviews charts, interprets them, and quickly recognizes changes in the direction of equity markets, they will be caught off guard**, leaving your investments in equities. You can quickly lose 20% of your investment value. That could be $100,000 in losses on a $500,000 and $200,000 on a $1 million portfolio. These losses could amount to 1 or 2 years, or more, of distributions when you are living off these funds. Avoiding these losses is critical. I minimized those losses with stops and kept market downturn losses to 5% or less.

7. **Rightly or wrongly, most investment advisory firms control your money and what you can do with it.** They tell you about your investments and when you can make them. They want your assets and yet tell you how your assets should be invested, usually in the advisory firm's products, the one where you have your investments. This message is self-serving, but they say they are helping you preserve your money. Sometimes this is true, mostly thought; it is selfish and focused on their needs and desires, not yours. No wonder there are five US firms with over a trillion in assets.

8. **If you do not regularly receive monthly investment newsletters, asset allocations, and reviews** of your investments monthly, with

benchmarks assigned to each portfolio to measure performance, then seek a new firm and a new advisor.

Chapter Four

INVESTMENT TRENDS, CHOICES, & RISK PROFILES

This chapter discusses financial goals, investment trends, investment choices, risk profiles, along with more discussion of asset allocation.

Financial Goals

First, why do you save? The short answer is to achieve your financial goals, such as owning a home, starting a business, retiring early, building a vacation home or primary home, building, buying, or selling a company, and/or giving millions [or billions] to your children and charities.

Financial advisors want to work with clients with financial assets and earnings, so they can focus on managing investments, evaluating insurance options, and performing equity analysis [reviewing equities for investment] to help you achieve your financial goals. Therefore, you need to have savings and income, be ready to name your financial goals, and allocate savings toward those goals with investments.

Significant Trends

What are the significant trends in investing for 2024?

1. **Passive investing**. Meaning that you buy indexes, for example, on the S&P500, that are not actively managed, meaning their performance is intended to mirror the S&P 500, without actively buying and selling stocks. It is like buying insurance to avoid

underperformance. Today, over 50% of passive investing is done with indexes in small-cap, mid-cap, and large-capitalization stocks. Passive investing iaccounts for over $12 trillion of assets in 2023,[21] and lowers the costs of investing, by lower fees, from lower transaction costs [less active management means less buying and selling].

2. **There are more ETFs than ever**, as ETF funds grew by 8552 new funds in 2021 and by 14,391 in 2022. ETF funds represent active management and lower annual costs than mutual funds, a continuing trend in the past few years. Total dollars invested in ETFs through December 31,2023 was $11.5 trillion.[22]

3. **ESG investing**, based on Environmental, Social, and Governance, has been popular politically and is gaining economic influence. It means that portfolio managers look out for opportunities to reduce the worldwide carbon print by investing low carbon energy, such as wind and solar, and investing in technology that reduces the use of oil and coal. ESG investments account for $7 trillion in assets.[23]

4. **401K assets are $6.9 trillion as of the 3rd quarter, 2023.[24]**

---

[21] Per morninstart chart, dated February 4, 2024, on website https://www.morningstar.com/funds/recovery-us-fund-flows-was-weak-2023

[22] Per Google search, February 5, 2024, ETFGI.com, website https://etfgi.com/news/press-releases/2023/12/assets-invested-etfs-industry-are-forecasted-hit-new-milestone-over-115

[23] Bloomberg, August 8th article, 2023, per Bloomberg website https://www.bloomberg.com/professional/blog/esg-funds-what-makes-for-good-performance/#:~:text=Environmental%2C%20Social%20and%20Governance%20(ESG,called%20out%20in%20their%20prospectus.

[24] Per Investment Company Institute, Google search dated February 4, 2024, for 401K assets and household assets https://www.ici.org/401k#:~:text=401(k)%20plans%20hold%20%246.9,of%20former%20employees%20and%20retirees.

5. Using **robots, or robo-advisors,** to automate portfolio management is estimated to grow near $1 trillion in the next few years.

6. **Total retirement assets** owned by US households, was $35.7 trillion by the 3rd quarter of 2023, with assets primarily invested in IRAs, $12.6 trillion, deferred compensation plans, $9.9 trillion, deferred benefit plans holding $11.1 trillion, and $2.2 trillion in annuity reserves.[25]

I will now discuss significant categories of investments. Know that you can spend years learning investments, and the following will provide a brief overview of investment assets, which may be candidates for investment in your investment portfolios.

In general, there are four types of investments offered in most investment accounts at advisory firms:

1. Cash
2. Bonds
3. Stocks & Equity Securities
4. Alternative investments

The categories of assets listed have increasing risk profiles as you move from cash to bonds, to stocks & equity securities, and to alternative investments, which are classified as the riskiest investments[but sometimes, they are not as risky as other assets, especially if they produce income]. Only investment types one to three above are offered in most 401k aeccounts. That is why Advisory firms and their advisors will suggest that you move assets out of a retirement account if you have moved to another firm and roll it into an IRA at their firm because of the broader range of investments available.

---

[25] Per the Investment Company Institute, February 4th, 2024 website, https://www.ici.org/statistical-report/ret_23_q3

Cash consists primarily of short-term securities, usually with a maturity of one year or less. It may include one-year Treasury securities, or 1-3 year ladder of Treasury securities, money market accounts, etc.

Bonds are longer-term investments, some of which offer coupons. They commonly have terms up to 30 years, some with terms up to 100 years. They usually offer a coupon, like a voucher, promising a specific payment to investors. Thus, it provides a specified rate of return. They are generally safe, depending on the creditworthiness of the company issuing the bonds. Lien holders have 1st lien upon the company's assets. Governments, a company, municipalities, and states may issue bonds. For example, municipal bonds are bonds issued by a city that may fund water or trash investments. Municipal bonds coupons [interest payments to you] are usually tax-free. That is a great benefit for high income earners to wish to invest and yet minimize taxes.

Stocks are equity investments with a risk of loss. You own a piece of the company, after bondholders are paid, and after preferred stock dividends are paid. If the company has excessive debt, this company could take bankruptcy, and only the bondholders, the lienholders of the company's assets, would get paid. That would mean stockholders could lose all of their investment.

Equity investments are generally classified into large-capitalization stocks, medium-capitalization stocks, small-capitalization stocks, international equities, and exchange-traded funds (ETFs) based on how large they are. Small-capitalization stocks usually range from $250 million to $2 billion in market capitalization, medium-capitalization stocks generally range in market value from $2 billion to $10 billion, and large-capitalization stocks range in value from $10 billion and up to $200 billion. You can also invest within each category, with value or growth. For example, small-cap value, mid-cap growth, etc.

Yet there are stocks with a market capitalization in the trillions: Google's market capitalization today [meaning Alphabet, ticker GOOG, dated February 4, 2024] is $1.756 trillion. I would call this group of stocks mega-cap stocks.

Other alternative assets could include investment partnerships in real estate, known as Real Estate Investment Trusts, and may invest in homes, shopping centers, or trees. You may qualify to invest in Initial Public Offerings (IPOs) of startup companies nearing profitability and thus have more significant growth opportunities than most investors.

You will have to be an **accredited investor** to invest in IPOs, and your income will have to be $200,000 or more if filing your taxes as single and $300,000 or more if married and filing jointly. Having this income will open more investment opportunities. But know that many of these opportunities are high-risk, and required significant due diligence before investing. Don't invest in these investments merely because your advisory firm underwrote them.

This category could also include crypto-currency, the purchase of various currencies, and any other high-risk investments. Most investors need to understand the risks of investing in crypto. Securities or other assets do not back most crypto: they are an alternative currency, but most, not all, are only partially supported by assets that retain their value.

So, some crypto investing is investing in air. Investopedia.com lists ten of the riskiest assets that are possible investment options. None of these investments will be available in a company-sponsored 401K program::

1. Options. For example, stock options on a company, the S&P 500 index, etc.

2. Futures, investing in commodities such as wheat, corn, and orange juice contacts.

3. Oil & gas drilling

4. Limited partnerships (real estate, usually)

5. Penny stocks

6. Alternative investments (this was my asset category # 4 above) can include art, collectibles (such as stamps), oil & gas drilling, leases, production, etc. Many of these are tax shelters and offer income and capital gains.

7. High-yield bonds (meaning high-interest rate, higher risk)

8. Leveraged ETFs (meaning money is borrowed to increase the investment

9. Emerging markets (say, a country fund in China, Russia, or Brazil.

10. Initial public offerings (IPOs). You need to be an accredited investor, thus, have an income of $200,000 per year if you file single status on your tax return or $300,000 per year if you file your income tax filing status if you file your taxes jointly.

The class of assets in asset class four, the riskier ones in real estate, and Initial Public Offerings (IPOs) will not be available as investment options in your company's 401K or pension fund. These investment assets generally require you to qualify for them by moving your IRA or 401K to an investment firm. However, I do not believe that markets are rational all the time, nor do I believe all alternative assets are riskier all the time. If you invest in producing timber or oil properties, and I think their risk is equal to or lower than investments in most oil companies: but it depends on the manager of the properties, and the property characteristics themselves, and that most of this information is non-public, thus harder to evaluate.

Risk Profiles
What is your risk profile?

Advisors will do their best to categorize you as an investor, usually asking you, as an investor, to complete a risk questionnaire. This questionnaire tells the advisor how much risk to take with your investments. They may classify you as an income investor, meaning low risk, and you primarily seek income from your investments. Another category would be a growth stock investor, for someone younger, with a higher risk profile, wanting to take more risk, say, in small capitalization stocks.

Most firms offering investments will place you, the investor, into one of five investment risk categories and then design portfolios that fit your profile.

The five most common investor risk profiles are:

1. **Conservative**. Usually, this is a risk-averse investor, investing only in cash and bonds.

2. **Moderately Conservative.** This investor primarily invests in cash, bonds, and some equity risk to fight inflation.

3. **Moderate**. This investor invests broadly in cash, bonds, and equity investments, usually with more emphasis on large-cap equities, and equities with dividends.

4. **Growth**. This investor is usually risk-seeking, investing primarily in equities and investments with above-average risk, and usually includes small-cap, mid-cap, and international stocks. Some investors in this category invest in all asset classes, which most likely depends on the investor's age.

5. **Aggressive.** This investor may be younger than many investors and has significant income and assets, so this person is a risk-seeking investor, who invests in all equity cap classes, international stocks, and are the best candidates for alternative investments.

You may be thinking: why would I ever invest in riskier assets like REITs, IPOs, or some special fund only available through Merrill Lynch or Blackrock?

I invested many of my growth investors into alternative assets. If you invest in all these categories of assets (all four), then you lower your overall portfolio risk. You might be investing minimal percentages of your portfolio, even for an income investor, but this reduces overall risk and increases returns. Why? Because the risk and return characteristics of alternative assets are not directed correlated to cash, bonds, or stocks.

And, if I had a moderate investor that had significant exposure to bonds, and thus interest rate risk, and if I was worried about inflation, and the Federal Reserve was raising interest rates, I would invest smaller amounts (than a growth investor, as a % of the portfolio) into these riskier assets, primarily to reduce risk and increase returns, especially if I can gain higher income in this investment than from the current portfolio investments stocks and bonds.

How do risky assets lower my overall portfolio risk? Asset classes 1-4 above react differently to economies and market events. So, if you own a portfolio of international stocks, and some economies are contracting while others are growing, this is a much safer investment than owning USA-based stocks only.

Why do you have some of your portfolios in cash? Cash is a risk reducer in the portfolio. Stock and bond investments can each reach peaks and be more likely to decline at certain times.

Bond prices decrease when interest rates are moving up, usually by the Federal Reserve, when credit quality is going down, when the currency the bond is issued in declines in value, or when the specific risk of this bond paying its coupon on time declines.

Stock prices may also decrease due to market bubbles, earnings declines, and other market events [Federal Reserve rates increases for example] that would have financed new investments for the company, or lower economic growth outputs for that country. Thus, there are many reasons for price declines. And sometimes, it would be better to have money in cash than to lose it when stock prices are declining. Think of cash as a hedge against losing money. You use it to lower the risk of investing in bonds or stocks, when markets are in decline.

Why should you invest some of your investment portfolio assets in bonds? When there is significant inflation, as there is now, and with lower than historical averages being paid on bonds, it is harder to invest 25% to 40% of your investment assets into bonds. Temporarily, based on market conditions, you may want a meager allocation to bonds, primarily because of inflation & interest rate risk reduce bond prices to decrease, and since interest rates are increasing [bond prices and interest rates move in opposite directions. Long-term bond returns before the past five years' cheap interest rates were 5%. Most bond investors are getting their returns "inflated" away. At present, there are minimal, if any real returns from bonds. What is the real rate of inflation? I don't know, and neither do most "experts."

Why own stocks? Because stocks can beat inflation and provide real returns over investing expenses. Stocks & real estate provide more significant opportunities to achieve long-term gains.

I suggest to my clients, with moderate and above risk tolerances, to own large-capitalization stocks, mid-capitalization stocks, and small-capitalization stocks and own positions in companies in stocks & ETFs,

including value and growth, in each category [large-mid-small-cap]. Choosing how much growth and how much value in each category should be performed by an investment expert, your advisor. That is what you hire them to do. Asset allocation is what they do when selecting how much to invest in each category of stocks or other investments.

More on Asset Allocation

So, what is asset allocation? It reflects the % of your investment portfolio invested in each asset category, adding to 100%. For example, for an investment portfolio, with a moderate risk tolerance:

1. Cash 10%. Your cash allocation is invested in short-term US Treasury securities for less than one year.

2. Bonds 25%. Your bond allocation is evenly split between Treasury, Municipal, and investment-quality company-issued bonds, with maturities of three to seven years.

3. Stocks & ETFs. 60% of your investment portfolio is split among large, medium, and small-capitalization stocks, value, and growth, with 10% allocated to international stocks.

4. Alternative investments. 5% in a REIT, whatever has been performing best within the real estate sector, or in an oil drilling & production partnership.

So this is an asset allocation. It tells you where your money will be invested and seeks diversification and appropriate investments for your risk tolerance. It needs to be adjusted, at least quarterly, & for large multi-million dollar investment portfolios, at least monthly.

Additionally, I suggest buying international stocks, with at least a moderate risk tolerance, when international equities are rising, or when economic growth in a specific country is growing faster than the US economy. There are country funds if you want to invest in a fast-growing economy, such as China or Thailand, or geographic-based funds that invest in Eastern Europe, Asia, or Africa. The returns are higher, but so is the risk.

Another category of international investments with significantly higher risk is emerging market funds. These funds invest in companies in faster-growing economies, which recently included the countries of China, Russia, Brazil, and India. If you invest in emerging markets, it is better, from a risk management point of view, to diversify and invest in a portfolio of companies in these countries.

What are some other risks or challenges to investing well?

There are three significant challenges to investing are inflation, US federal debt, & taxes.

One underrated issue is inflation. What happens to your financial plan if inflation exceeds most investment returns in bonds and equities? Equities and real estate are usually used in financial and investment strategies to beat inflation.

Know that the US government's reported rates of inflation are overly low. They say inflation was, for example, 3% when it was likely 7% to 10%, in the past few years, in 2020-2023. Why do they do that? Well, governments want to say they are doing a good job. No US president likes to say he is doing a terrible job with the economy. So, this is a common lie. The CPI [consumer price index] does not give a true measure of inflation.

Think about how destructive inflation is to your portfolio: if your portfolio makes 10% this year, but inflation is 8%, you only gained 2%. That is not much of a gain. I say this because the US has printed so much money in the last few years [$20 trillion] that, regardless of who is President, inflation will be higher than you or I planned.

Fighting the adverse effects of inflation requires more risk management tools in your investment portfolio to hedge interest rates in your bond portfolios and inflation risks in your bond and equity portfolios. Your advisor needs to address these risks more profoundly than ever. Will they use options or futures to hedge your interest rate risk? Does your financial advisor or firm have the skills and experience to do this? Will your advisory firm allow you to do this? The **bottom line** is that only some firms have the products, skills, and structures to manage these investment risks and offer them to their private wealth clients. **Make sure** that you have such a firm and such an advisor.

A primary cause of inflation in the United States is the dramatic increase in debt [printed money] since 2000. In September 2000, the US federal debt was $5.7 trillion. Ten years later, by September 2010, this exact debt figure was $13.7 trillion. By February 4, 2024, the US federal debt was $34.155 trillion. The US Federal Government used the historically lower borrowing rates of the past ten years [2013 to 2022] to fund crushing amounts of debt. The US federal debt has increased 249% (using simple math) in the last 13 years and over 599% during the previous 22 years (again, simple math). Those increases need to be more sustainable. Borrowing this much money is not sustainable, no matter how low-interest rates are.

How long can you borrow more than your yearly income? That is what the US has been doing for some time now. **Why? Other nations and their investors will not continue to buy US debt.** The US can only sustainably borrow up to its income yearly and continue to import $537 billion of goods from China annually. Eventually, the US debt would crowd out all other long-term bond investments. Until the US is declared bankrupt for its debt, when it can no longer pay with historically higher interest rates, it will likely have continuously higher inflation and taxes. Right now, the US government is having budgeting problems: it can no longer pay for Social Security and Medicare and pay for defense without cutting one or the other. Cuts to the US budget are needed: I would not want social security or medicare benefits cut. These changes are coming, and most investors must prepare for them. Governments threatened by bankruptcy could nationalize the assets of companies & investors. That is a real risk with the US national debt.

The US federal government may be required to balance its budget by the financial market's more austere conditions, such as inflation, taxes, possible bankruptcy, and potentially a new currency. These patterns cannot continue for long. That will affect all US investors and could plunge the US economy into depression for a decade or more. That would severely damage every US citizen's finances, & especially stock and bond portfolios. These issues of inflation, debt, and taxes will significantly influence investing and your investment values for the next 25 years.

How will these issues impact your portfolio? An extremely critical issue in investing is the tax structure of your investment vehicle. Most clients accumulate money in IRAs, which are taxable when you take cash out. Let's say you earn $3 million in your IRA: and you assume that you will have 35% taxes. What happens if taxes are 50%? Well, it blows up your plan. No advisor in existence can predict what future tax rates will be. Estimating future tax rates is like shooting darts: you rarely hit the bullseye, and mostly you guess.

The federal government has printed a significant amount of money in the US due to deficits, COVID, and poor economic performance. The national debt is $34.155 trillion, more than the US GDP in 2023, which was $27.36 trillion. If you understand what I have said about inflation, taxes, & debt, you will likely face much higher taxes than in the past. That makes tax-free investing worth more, or in taxable now structures, as the taxes have been paid, instead of in future tax scenarios like IRAs. A good IRA would be a ROTH IRA: you don't get deductions when you invest in one, but when you take money out, you get credit for your contributions. Even a taxable investment account is superior to a regular IRA when you take distributions, as you have a basis for your assistance.

Most of my clients had accumulated money in their 401Ks and IRAs. That is smart. But it is also intelligent to have funds in tax-free and tax-now structures to minimize taxes in the future. If income taxes increase on all income plus investments, which is likely, then you will lower your overall tax. If you have paid taxes on income and then invested, and if you hold stocks and bonds for a year or more, you have capital gains, which is generally a lower rate than tax rates on income. So, start investing in a tax-free or tax-now structure (taxable investment account vs. an IRA) instead of waiting for income taxes to go up on your IRA, where the income taxes could be much higher.

Another vital lesson from investing for my clients was that most clients need to know when to get out of equities when equities are likely to fall 20% or more in a year. It was clear from my investment research at Merrill and Woodbury that equities would fail in some years due to the economic outlook, housing sector, poor company earnings, and inflation. Advisors should know when to do this and then do it for clients. If your advisor cannot do this, they should be doing something else.

Saving a fall in equities of 20% in portfolios can make the difference of 2-3 years of accumulation. That is what you risk when you stay in equities when equity markets are falling. And when the downturn is over, which is usually clear from charts, such as stockcharts.com, it is time to go with a 70% or 80% equity allocation and make more money than the S&P 500. Doing these two things can increase your investment savings by 7-10 years and allow you, the investor, to retire earlier or with more money. Isn't that the name of the game?

Too many advisors promote their returns but need to adjust for risk. Quantitative analysis can be performed on any portfolio using the

Sharpe ratio. You can Google the exact formula. The formula takes the return of an asset you plan to add to your portfolio. You subtract from this the risk-free rate of investment (say that return on a five- or ten-year treasury bond) and divide this by the standard deviation of the asset you plan to invest. Not all clients are risk-seeking investors. And many advisors promote their returns without adjusting for risk.

You can calculate the Sharpe ratio for any portfolio and any asset. Use this for your portfolio overall and for any new recommendations that are significantly higher risk than the positions you already own in your portfolio. Google the Sharpe ratio and learn more about that as a measure of portfolio risk.

Only invest in products or investment structures [such as IRAs, Roth IRAs, Taxable investment accounts] [or insurance policies] that you understand. Ensure you know the potential gains and likely risks for every investment. Start out investing in cash, bonds, stocks, and ETFs. Keep learning about investments, and seek to gain reasonable returns for the risks that you take. Be careful with options and futures: you can gain significant amounts, and you can also lose all of your investments, and even more with futures. If you become an expert in options and futures, you will be rewarded for investing your time to be an expert.

How to reduce investment risks in stocks and investing:
How can you reduce the risks of investing? One strategy I used for my retirement investors was to put 5% stop orders [which are sell orders which reduce the risk of loss] on all stock and ETF investments. It helped me communicate with clients; I was serious about risk management. I told clients that the most they could lose is 5% in any position.

It worked very well. During volatile times, we had a few positions get stopped [meaning the market volatility caused the stop to be hit, and the position was sold automatically]. But 99.9% of the time, it was successful and reduced risk.

How can you minimize risks in investing in bonds? I would talk to your advisor and consider investing in interest-rate options or futures than make you money when interest rates go up. I would only do this with significant assets committed to bonds, say $1 million or more. I would discuss this with an advisor who is a specialist in bonds, or has a bond specialist available to them within their firm.

Chapter Five

MY RECOMMENDATIONS ABOUT INVESTMENTS

This chapter discusses products, advisory firm's product lines, challenges to investing, including inflation, US federal debt, and taxes, some advice on fees and what products you purchase.

What is a good product line for investments?

1. **A fee-based advisory account that limits fees to solely an account fee** between 1% and 2 % per year for most investment accounts. If the assets are $1-10 million, then a fee likely below 1%.

2. **Access to 99% of all small-, medium-, and large-capitalization stocks,** and the same for Exchange-traded funds, including some funds that manage interest rate and equity downturn risks, that allow shorting of certain positions temporarily to manage client investment risks, primarily in stocks and bonds.

3. **For retirement accounts, I like annuities**. You will hear many investors argue about whether they are good. You primarily accumulate funds in your investment fee-based advisory account, but an annuity is the best distribution vehicle. Most have income guarantees and encourage you to take higher investment risks due to the assurances about the investment values. When clients are ready to take distributions, annuities offer guaranteed income and ability to take distributions & flexibility not available from an investment account.

4. **Arguments about annuities are primarily focused on fees**. I agree that annuities are expensive accumulation vehicles: but I used them primarily as distribution vehicles. I gained guarantees that no one has over any investment portfolio in terms of investment values and fixed balances to pay income over time, guaranteeing a certain income level, which is only possible in investment accounts with options and hedges. For example, if you invest $300,000 in an annuity, and it gains investment value to $400,000, many annuities allow you to lock in the highest gains for income distribution purposes and take 5% of that, with an income of $20,000. **Do any investment accounts guarantees your values for income distribution?** No, none. Annuities are a good deal when used correctly, primarily for distribution. And when equity markets are declining, that is an excellent way to get guarantees and lower investment risks, especially when a client feels beaten up by equity market performance and needs a psychological boost. Annuities are valuable then also. Most people who say annuities are not worth it don't understand them, don't manage money, look only at fees & not the guarantees inside the investment, or lack investment expertise. Ignorance likes to talk.

5. **Alternative investments allow you, the investor, to diversify risk further and gain income and capital gains**, notably REITS, [Real Estate Investment Trusts], timber, oil and gas drilling, etc. You may not want or need them now, but it is better to have them available than not. I used timber and oil and gas to diversify some clients, in addition to owning oil and gas stocks. The income investments had lower risk, higher income, and were a fundamentally different investment vehicle, concerning its risk and return properties, than oil and gas stocks or ETFs.

6. **Gold and silver must be purchased privately unless you purchase through ETFs.** Due to inflation and taxes, I would look for

every opportunity to make money. In this current environment of slower economic growth, high US debt, and high inflation [2023 and 2024], silver and gold investments can help you gain returns above inflation. You can buy ETFs, such as SLV for silver and IAU for Gold. You can also purchase coins of silver and gold. If you buy silver or gold coins, make sure you are dealing with a reputable dealer and have multiple vendors so you can be sure you have a good deal. The only negative about buying gold and silver coins is that you have to store them. In the 1940s, the US government confiscated gold from safe deposit boxes. So, you will want to keep them somewhere else. You will figure that out for yourself.

7. **Options have tremendous value in reducing investment risks when equity indexes, such as the S&P 500, have peaked.** You can decrease equity allocations and buy a put on the market. If you need help understanding this, get a book on options and read it. Also, in the early stage of an equity market upturn, buying options on the market [purchasing a call, say on the S & P] can dramatically increase your gains. But you or your advisor need to be experts to do this well. Find an advisor to do this for you, or learn options yourself. Your long-term financial success may depend upon this knowledge and expertise, such as hedging, buying and selling calls, as many firms will not offer this to private investors, unless they have $10 million or more in investable assets.

Most of my clients had accumulated money in their 401Ks and IRAs. That is smart. But it is also intelligent to have funds in tax-free and tax-now structures to minimize taxes in the future. If income taxes increase on all income plus investments, which is likely, then you will lower your overall tax by investing in ROTH IRAs and taxable investment accounts. If you have paid taxes on income and then invested, and if you hold stocks and bonds for a year or more, you have capital gains, which is generally a lower rate than tax rates on income. So, start investing in a tax-free or tax-now structure (taxable investment account vs. an IRA, and ROTH accounts) instead of waiting for income taxes to go up on your IRA, where the income taxes could be much higher.

Another vital lesson from investing for my clients was that most clients need to know when to get out of equities, when equities are more likely to fall 20% in a year, than go up. It was clear from my investment research at Merrill and Woodbury that equities would fail in some years due to the economic outlook, housing sector, poor company earnings, and inflation. Advisors should know when to do this and then do it for clients. If your advisor cannot do this, or do not know how to discern this, then they should be doing something else, and you should be looking for an advisor who can do this.

Preventing a fall in equities of 20% in retirement portfolios can make the difference of 4-5 years of accumulation. That is what you risk when you stay in equities when equity markets are falling. And when the downturn is over, which is usually clear from charts, such as stock-charts.com, it is time to go with a 70% or 80% equity allocation and make more money [when markets are rising] than the S&P 500. Doing these two things can increase your investment savings by 7-10 years and allow you, the investor, to retire earlier or with more money. Isn't that the name of the game?

Another important topic in investing is fees.

I offer the following advice on the costs of investing and when & why I choose certain investments at certain times:

1. **Due to the low costs of investing in ETFs [exchange-traded funds], buy ETFS and hold them unless you can identify a superior portfolio manager** [think Peter Lynch in the 1980s and 1990s, and Warren Buffett]. You should always invest in lower costs structures, like stocks and ETFs. Most mutual funds have fees of 1.5% to

3% or more. Most of them underperform and are not worth your investment. If that is your only choice in your 401k, invest in those, but outside of your company investment 401k, try to use lower-cost structures, such as ETFs. Mutual funds are suitable for the fund companies who create them, [and very profitable for them] but rarely are they the best vehicle for an investor who can qualify for better management and lower fees. Again, mutual funds were important when they offered diversification and professional management an investor could not get elsewhere: now they are one of the worst examples of investing, with higher costs & lower performance. Who needs that? Mutual funds are dinosaurs currently being replaced by ETFs, lower costs, better diversification, and the replacement of below-average portfolio managers.

2. **I think about investments like this in terms of costs:** if you can invest in ETFs to get the exposure, return, and risk, and use, for example, an S&P 500 ETF, instead of buying the top 50 performing stocks out of that index. You have exposure to 500 of the most extensive stocks in the US and multiple industries, and you have the lowest cost of investing. What could be better than that? [I would make this decision based on long-term performance of the S & P 500 ETF and the top fifty stocks within the ETF]. There are mid-cap indexes also. Saving 1% or more on investment expenses is the same as earning 1% more in your investment returns. Do everything you can to lower your fees. 1% per year accumulates over time. If you save 1% for 30 years, you will have substantially boosted your investment portfolio. Get rid of mutual funds outside of your company's 401K, and if you can avoid mutual funds in your company's 401k, do so.

3. **I buy stocks when they outperform their index by 2% or more quarterly** [a growth perspective] or if their value is substantially more than equity markets currently value them [a value

perspective]. Those two reasons are the primary reasons to buy stocks. Buy what is going up. And I put a 5% stop on all equity investments, so if fundamentals or technical trends change and they fall, [fast-growing stocks can drop quickly if their earnings slow], this will not significantly impact your portfolio. Why else should you buy stocks? You purchase stocks for overperformance, not for underperformance. Buying the S&P 500 index insures your portfolio against underperformance. You buy the "overperformers" to get more returns while putting 5% stocks on them [possibly higher stops for these stocks] to manage investment risk. Additionally, in years where stocks are only appreciating 7% to 10% per year, investing in income-producing stocks, for example, oil companies that have a dividend, can improve your returns by 3-4%. That is a significant increase in years when performance is harder to achieve. Bottom line: buy what is performing, look for long term trends. I did this by reviewing long term charts.

4. **I prefer to buy small-capitalization stocks only when they over-perform**. The NASDAQ 100 QQQM [ticker] index had a value of $232.87 billion, while the S&P 500 index ishare IVV had a value on this same date of $399 billion. Investing more money in the S&P makes more sense, which offers more diversification and has less risk of loss during most market conditions. It is better to pick and choose among small stocks that grow much faster than large companies when they are outperforming the S&P 500 but have more risk. I would use my firm's research or a software investment research program like Vectorvest.com, which can identify fast-growing companies. And I would put stops on these investments, between 5 % and 10%. If you have a good advisor, get them to research small-cap stocks, make recommendations on buying or not and get their recommendations on stops.

5. **I would own Berkshire Hathaway stocks, BRK.A**. This gives you an opportunity for overperformance above the S&P 500 stock index. I know this is not pure diversification over it, but this is one of the best portfolio managers in the country, with concentrated stock positions. Overperformance in stocks comes from less diversified portfolios, as the more diversified you are, the more likely you have diversified away from the best performers. If you have invested in the S&P500 index already, which insures against underperformance, this is the best way I know, other than options on specific stocks, to out perform the S&P 500. And if you do options, you still have to select the specific positions to buy or sell options.

6. **For international stocks, I would use my firm's research**, talk to your advisor, and do some research with Vectorvest.com. These stocks or ETFs are riskier than S&P 500 stocks and require risk management. Again I would use stops. I would look at the small-cap and international stocks as a group, identify the best performers worth investing in, and then decide on an asset allocation based on my firm's research and the quality of the investment opportunities available in small-cap and international stocks.

7. **I buy alternative investments when it diversifies risk**, has significant long-term capital gain potential, and when these investments can provide income when a client is distributing his assets [taking distributions from say, an IRA]. Suppose a client has done significant accumulation and is taking income. In that case, I think about an annuity to guarantee his ability to take income and get benefits that this investor cannot get from his investment account. There are no guarantees when you have achieved your accumulation goal [$ amount to achieve before taking distributions] that your account balance will retain its value, when you are taking distributions over a long time period.

75

8. **I would do regular research on the clean energy sector, low-carbon investing**, and research into using oil and coal more efficiently. This sector is popular & called the ESG sector, known as Environmental, Social, and Governance investing. Global investment into this sector was $501 billion in 2020, $755 billion in 2021, and $1.1 trillion in 2022, per Reuters. Look for 10X in the improvement & efficiency of the technology to help buyers change their investment habits [recommendation, Peter Thiel, in his book, Zero to One], or else the change needs to be more significant. When solar power & wind turbine technology can increase by a magnitude of 10X where they started, that is when clean energy will produce more substantial investment returns. So far, the returns, when compared to the investment, have been poor. The only successful clean energy company is Tesla. Look for companies that dominate small niches first [also a suggestion of Peter Thiel, in his book **Zero to One**]. No one company is going to dominate global energy, a multi-trillion-dollar industry. However, one company will most likely lead in solar, wind, or new power generation. Look for public companies that dominate niches and have strong intellectual property protection. Because their technology and value will draw copycats from everywhere, Make sure that you are investing for actual returns, not because it is socially or politically popular, but because it makes real returns beyond inflation, taxes, and investing expenses.

9. **I recommend buying options or futures when equity markets are shifting directions, firmly up or down**. Again, you may have to do this in your private investment accounts, not with an advisor. It would be best to do this with an advisor. Make sure you have good investment research and know what you are doing. Know this is a risky move, but it can pay huge returns. These significant shifts show up in charts with 100-day and 200-day moving averages on

the major indexes, such as the S&P 500 and Nasdaq 100 Composite, and are reflected clearly on charts, such as those by Stockcharts.com. When the 50 day moving average of any major index breaks the 100 day moving average, that is a buy signal. Talk with your advisor and decide when you will invest in other areas that may not be performing right now: have a buy signal for international stocks, small stocks, etc.

10. **Only invest in products or investment structures [such as IRAs, Roth IRAs, Taxable investment accounts] [or insurance policies] that you understand**. Ensure you know the potential gains and likely risks for every investment. Start out investing in cash, bonds, stocks, and ETFs. Keep learning about investments, and seek to gain reasonable returns for the risks that you take. Be careful with options and futures: you can gain significant amounts, and you can also lose all of your investment, and even more with futures. If you become an expert in options and futures, I believe that you will be rewarded for investing your time to be an expert.

Criteria that drove my equity and ETF choices:

1. **Faster growing economies,** stable & democratic, than the US or Western Europe. I never invested in Russia or Iran.

2. **Stock and equities in sectors that are performing now**. I always learned to be on top of sector performance, which creates significant opportunities to make money when they change.

3. **Faster growth in earnings** than averages in the S&P 500.

4. **Lower risk** than the S&P 500 market index.

5. **Usually, this was manufacturing, energy, & financial stocks**, some retail, and very few technology companies. I liked the large

oil production stocks for their dividends under challenging markets. They stabilized my clients' portfolios during those times.

6. **I like technology.** But you need to understand what you are investing in: What is the technology, and how strong is the intellectual property protection?

7. **Most investors need to understand more completely, the technology stocks they own.** Sometimes their IP goes away, and another company has upstaged them. I would not recommend avoiding technology; understand the risks and returns of what you are investing in.

Chapter Six

Insurance Helps Manage Risk

Insurance helps you manage risk . For example, property insurance on your home and automobiles protect their value in case of storms, accidents, damages, etc. Insurance here protects your investments in your home and cars. Instead of losing your investment when injuries to their value occur, you get them repaired or acquire new ones.

Life insurance replaces the family's income in case one of the wage earners' dies so that the family can avoid financial hardship. Everyone with a home or automobile should have property insurance. In almost all states in the US, automobile insurance is required [except for New Hampshire]. Life insurance also raises essential matters: what do you want to happen if you die? Who do you want to inherit your property? What do you want to happen for your children if you pass away? Who would be their caretakers if you and your wife have a tragic accident?

Life insurance statistics. Approximately 52% of Americans have life insurance, and 30% of US citizens aged 42-76 own their life insurance policies, while 22% of Americans aged 42-76 have life insurance only through work. 8 out of 10 consumers in the US overestimate the cost of life insurance. About 44% of American households would encounter significant hardship by losing the primary wage earner.[26]

---

[26] Google search, February 7th, 2024, Forbes Advisor web site, article "Life Insurance Statistics, Data and Industry Trends, 2023".

Here is an example of a primary wage-earner, who earns $200,000 per year, is 50 years old, married, and has three children. This couple wants to save ten more years to meet retirement goals and wants $500,000 to finance their children's college education. To simplify our example, we will assume that this family has the proper amounts of property, long-term care, and health insurance. This family wants to buy a life insurance policy, to ensure that if the primary wage earner dies prematurely, the family can educate the children and the spouse has the money to finance retirement. Most advisors suggest between $2 million and $3 million of insurance to fund living expenses, education, and retirement goals. Due to the cost, this life insurance is likely a term life policy.

If there is a non-working spouse in this example, the couple would also get a life insurance policy to ensure the care of the children if the homemaker dies prematurely. So, let's say the cost of a full-time person to care for the children would be $50,000 per year, and then children would need that for ten years, then this family would seek a $500,000 life insurance policy on the non-working spouse.

Most people attempt to avoid considering these possibilities. These are complicated issues; and too many clients want to deny this can happen. Life insurance is necessary if you wish to care for your loved ones. It requires thought about what most of us want to avoid considering.

Additionally, suppose you were involved in an accident and declared guilty of causing an accident and permanent damage [such as a victim being unable to walk again or there was a death]. In that case, this could be a multi-million dollar judgment against you, possibly a prison sentence. To protect yourself and your family against such a tragedy, drive safely and carry insurance on your home and your automobiles. Let your property insurance agent recommend the coverages.

Long-term care insurance pays for elder care when someone needs care daily or helps with one of six daily living activities. If you or your loved ones need long-term care, that can quickly exhaust your savings. In most places in the US, long-term care is $100,000 per year or more. So, five years of this can easily use up $500,000 of your assets. These policies are costly.

Know that the maximum Medicare will pay for the first 100 days of elder care. After that, only long-term care insurance and your savings will pay for it unless you are in a hospital for three days, then Medicare will pay for the first 100 days again, or at least 80% of that, depending on specific requirements. Don't expect Medicare to pay for long-term care for you or a family member.

Some of my clients did "elder care planning" [without my advice] to take assets out of the name of the person going into elder care so that they could claim poverty and the inability to pay for the maintenance [hiding millions of dollars of assets elsewhere]. Thus, states and Medicaid end up paying for this care. But states are getting wiser, and after this person dies and their heirs inherit their property, states return with lawyers, fighting in court, for the money they paid for elder care, interest, and legal fees. In most states, unless the person is genuinely unable to pay for care, don't bother with "elder care planning." You and your family must figure out how to pay for elder care.

If your parents or grandparents died in their 80s, 90, or 100s due to the longevity in your family, you should strongly consider long-term care insurance. Also, if you have had family members go to elder care facilities, you should strongly consider buying a long term care policy. I recommend getting a quote for three to five years of long-term care. The earlier you think about this, the better, as these policies get more expensive in your 50s and 60s. Why? Think of this as insuring your assets, your home, investments, etc, against catastrophe.

Long-term Care Statistics

The likelihood of a 70-year-old female needing long-term care is 5.6%; at age 80, it is 27.20%, and at age 90, it is 58.3%.[27] .So, instead of assuming that you or your spouse do not need long-term care insurance, consider buying long-term care insurance in your forties or fifties rather than later.

The likelihood of a 70-year-old male needing long-term care is 5.3%; at age 80, 24.3%, and age 90, 51.10%.[28] [also quoted from The American Association for Long-Term Care Insurance, 2022 statistics, www. aaltci.org.

Most of my clients still needed to buy it or have savings to pay for long-term care. You will not know if you need it: having it would be better than having elder care costs consume your investment portfolio. I offered this insurance to my clients, but only a few were willing to consider it.

So, over 50% of the investing population should prepare for elder care [based on statistics above for women and men needing care] **which could blow up their financial plans.** I hope you don't need it, but more than 50% of the US population will likely need elder care. I am the messenger here, telling you that you and your family may need it. I hope that elder care does not negatively impact your financial plans. Also, know that other insurance, such as health insurance, does not pay for elder care.

Speaking of health insurance, ensure you have health insurance coverage at work or get a health insurance policy. The lack of health

---

[27] Google search, February 7, 2024, The American Association for Long-Term care insurance., 2022 statistics, at their website, www.aaltci.org, statistics for women needing long-term care.

[28] Google search dated February 7th, 2024, from The American Association for Long-Term Care insurance, 2022 statistics at www.aaltci.org, statistics for men.

insurance causes many financial problems, from hospital bills to burial costs and economic hardship for family members. Better to pay for this than leave your family with unpaid bills and without a wage earner. Enough said.

Health insurance statistics

According to The National Center for Health Statistics, reporting for 2022 stated that of adults in the US ages 18-64, 68.1% had private health insurance, 21.8% had public coverage, and 12.1% were uninsured. Twenty-seven million people of all ages were uninsured.

Another area of risk is disability insurance, which replaces income if you are hurt or unable to work for an extended period of time. At Guardian Insurance, we commonly recommended a three or five-year disability policy, which would replace the income you would have earned from work, yet were unable to because of health issues.

Disability insurance statistics

9.2 million Americans received disability income payments in 2022, per the Social Security Administration. The **Center for Disease Control** reports that 61 million Americans have some disability; they say that the most common types of disabilities are motor skills and cognition skills.

How can you use Life insurance to build wealth?

1. **Purchase more insurance** than your family needs to replace the primary wage-earners' income and pay bills and final expenses. Include money to pay for children's education, elementary, secondary, and college. The younger you are, the better, as it costs much more to add insurance coverage after ages 50. Leave the money to heirs such as husbands, wives, children, etc. If they are young, put the money into a trust, and assign trustees. Most people consider life insurance a necessary evil, but life insurance can be utilized to

build wealth. You can use it for your family to buy investments, real estate, and businesses.

2. **Life insurance can be used to create your own family bank**. Let's say you are in your 20s or 30s and want to invest. If equity markets are declining, why not put that money into a $100,000 or $250,000 whole-life insurance policy? Then overfund it, up to the limit [IRS rules govern how much you can put into an insurance policy]. These policies pay dividends and are tax-free up to the value of your contributions. You can quickly build this up to having $100,000 or more in cash available for borrowing, which you can put into real estate, businesses, or other investments. Why not do this when equity markets are falling, you need life insurance anyway, and then you have a private bank you can borrow from at any time? You must repay these funds, but your borrowing rate will be less than at banks. Over your lifetime, you could easily have $500,000 n this account, ready for you to use, and its distribution is tax-free, up to the value of your contributions. I have used this to reduce the risk that future IRA distributions [not ROTH] will be at much higher tax rates. Most of the value of this investment in insurance distributes tax-free. You cannot say that about a 401K or IRA [not Roth].

3. **Overfund a whole-life policy for your child** between the ages of 1-10. By the time they are age 18, ready for a career, they can likely have $100,000 or more to use for education, starting a business, or buying a business or real estate. No financial instrument is more flexible than this [other than a taxable investment account] in terms of low taxes and the ability to purchase almost anything. The over-funded life insurance policy is 10X better than a 529 education plan, which has fewer investment options, is tightly controlled, and needs the greater flexibility of the investment account or over-funded whole life policy.

4. **People who want to argue about buying life insurance are usually reason that investments earn a better rate of return.** My response is that only some things are about the rate of return. First, you and everyone else will die, so why not benefit your heirs? Second, life insurance lowers risk for a client by addressing a real need. Third, there are tax benefits. Fourth, creating your own bank by over-funding a whole life policy is flexibility most people only have within a taxable investment account, meaning this account cannot be an IRA or Roth IRA. Fifth, most people who argue about the rate of return do not understand their investment risks, and most have not addressed their insurance risks concerning health, life, long-term care, and disability insurance. Most arguments about whole-life insurance do not address the risk of investments: whole-life insurance is much safer. If you have managed your insurance risks, then whole-life is adding to lowering the risk of your investment portfolio. Investment risks should be minimized, not maximized.

Other insurance options

There is also term insurance. I like term insurance for being cheap, but you still need insurance when you are 65. Even when you are 65, you want the money that pays your final expenses, any bills or debts, and gives money to your heirs tax-free. Insurance can be a family wealth builder, if you purchase it early in life rather than later. Most clients only have life insurance from their employer, which changes every time they change jobs. It is better to have some permanent family owned insurance, that survives job changes and employment. Many family benefit from having a stable source of insurance.

When you are older, say 55-65, cheap term insurance becomes expensive term. Whole life insurance costs more to start, but you buy earlier in life, and retain this policy over the long term, it lowers your overall risk, and diversified some risk of taxes on your IRA distributions.

Another option is Variable Life Insurance. With high investment expenses, this insurance invests in the provider's mutual funds. You can build significant wealth if your investments do well, but if the investments do poorly your insurance policy lapses. I know many advisors who sell this for clients, primarily for the high commission it pays advisors. If you can buy this at the start of a business cycle, you can do very well here, if equity gains end up paying for your insurance. But only if the investments are managed well, do you retain your life insurance. This is risky and not what I would recommend for most people.

Please let me explain. The Investment accounts [within the variable life insurance policy] support the insurance (VUL). If the investment values go up, the policy may be self-supporting, meaning you don't have to put more money in premiums in the policy. However, if the investment values go down, the policy breaks, and the policy owner needs to put up more money than the typical premium to keep the policy in force. So, VUL policies must be closely watched so that investments can be changed if they are not gaining value from the investments.

In my experience, most Variable Life Insurance policies' investment accounts could be reviewed more closely, more often, by an investment expert. Not paying attention to the investments causes significant problems, as the investments support the policy. To be clear, if the investments in a VUL policy lose money, the owners must either put down more money to support the premium or forfeit the life insurance policy. You need your insurance to be in force, not subject to equity market performance.

In losing a life insurance policy on a wage earner, the negative consequences here are caused because the salesman, who is usually more of an insurance advisor and not knowledgeable about investments, assumed he did not have to review these investments. These policies only work well when you gain value in equity markets for at least a couple of years and overfund your premium, paying more than the minimum required to start the policy. And they only work well when you have an advisor who is good at investments and manages them. Since these investments are in your insurance company's mutual funds, you cannot use risk management tools, such as putting sell orders if any position drops 5%.

So two things are at work here. Usually this is sold by an insurance salesman who is bad at investments, or not knowledgeable enough to manage the investments inside the policy. And families need insurance policies to be stable and in force. Unless you are confident that you are investing early into a strong, rising equity market and have an advisor who is a good investor and carefully monitors the performance of your investments, then buy term or whole life insurance. I prefer whole life insurance, but primarily I care that my clients have life insurance. Term policies, at minimum, are stable and stay in force as long as the premium on your insurance is paid. Please review all your options on life insurance before buying, getting quotes on term, whole life, and Variable Life Insurance. Your choice should be based on benefits, costs, and who is there to manage these policies.

My Advice

1. **Have your property insurance agent review your automobile and home insurance policies** to see if they can offer additional discounts. If these policies are in one place, you will receive 20-30% discounts for your property insurance. Most of the time, your property insurance experts can get more bang for your buck, and improve your overall coverage, when you ask them to review your policies. If your property agent is sleepy and does not make recommendations, then find another one.

2. **I recommend that all homeowner clients have an umbrella policy on their home insurance** for $1 million [at least] to protect

themselves from any lawsuits or accidents at their homes. If this happened to you without this insurance, an accident or lawsuit could cost you all your life savings. So, getting an umbrella policy protects your investments, income, and family from hardships. I own a farm and carry the umbrella policy to defend myself against any accidents that could occur on the farm. I am insuring and protecting my net worth. Umbrella policies reduce risks and are cheap when added to home & auto insurance policies.

3. **Get quotes on long-term care insurance** for you and your spouse, regardless of age. Knowing what it might cost you is better than assuming you can't afford it. If your net worth is above $10 million, then you can pay for it out of cash. Most clients need help paying for long-term care insurance.

4. **Think about what you want to happen for your family if you die young**. Get quotes on life insurance for you and your spouse if you are married. Establish a will or trust, where you specify what you want to have to happen if you die. I am for you, living long and healthy. Just know that does not happen for everyone, and it is better to make plans than have this wreck your family's finances for the long term.

5. **Get quotes on disability insurance for three to five years if you are single or married.** If you are single, that protects your extended family members from having to pay your bills if you cannot work, and if married, this will protect your family from loss of income if you cannot work.

6. **Know that you should handle your insurance risks before investing substantial funds long-term.** By all means, you should invest. Most of my clients needed to pay more attention to large areas of risks within the insurance category. Not addressing risks that insurance can eliminate or substantially reduce is a common

mistake. Few advisors review all your insurance plans [or know enough do that] to ensure that you have addressed the significant risks. The better advisors will be knowledgeable in health, life, long-term care, and disability insurance, or have experts in the firm that can review your policies.

7. **Warning: most investment firms have advisors who should be more skilled in life insurance and long-term care insurance and thus cannot give you expert advice for insurance**. They have insurance licenses and can sell them, but only a few are experts. Life insurance firms with advisors are experts in life and long-term care insurance and are more likely to give you the expertise you need as you approach your life insurance, long-term care, and estate planning issues in your financial plan. As an advisor with Guardian life insurance, I was trained significantly in life and long-term care insurance and financial planning. And I had full-time experts who would help me quote life insurance, long-term care, and disability insurance.

8. **For example, At Merrill Lynch, 99% of advisors were investment experts.** In our Galleria branch of Merrill Lynch, there were 50 advisors, and I did not know of any experts in life or long-term care insurance. I was an investment expert there. Few advisors are experts in more than one area. That is why some advisors have teams with insurance experts. As an advisor with Guardian Life, I became much better informed about life and long-term care insurance. You should talk to an insurance expert when deciding on life, disability, & long-term care insurance or estate planning issues.

9. **I offered each of my clients advice on these critical areas of insurance:** disability, long-term care, life, health, retirement planning, and estate planning. Many investment clients turned me down and wanted to keep that private. And the clients that

allowed me the opportunity to review all their insurance, financial plans, and estate plans, we got to know each other better. The result was that I improved their insurance coverage according to their means, my clients were better informed about risks, and I could perform better with their investments, as I was more informed about their goals, plans, means, and decision-making about risks. There are benefits to financial transparency, when you work with an advisor that you trust.

10. **Make sure you are talking to experts about insurance.** Let experts inform you about life, health, disability, and long-term care insurance. First, I would focus on health and life insurance, save money, and then address disability and long-term care. I would not let most insurance experts manage my investments, and I would not let investment advisors offer me insurance., But that is how I see it. **Ensure you understand the background(s) of the person(s)** offering you investment and insurance advice. Are they qualified to offer that advice? Do they have experts in these areas backing them up?

Storytime

I always reviewed my client's insurance policies and referred them to their property insurance advisor to raise coverage on autos and get an umbrella policy. Too many people live in cities and yet only have $100,000 in liability coverage and $100,000 in property damage on their automobiles. You will likely exceed those limits if you own a Mercedes and hit a Lexus. Talk to your property insurance agent and discuss your automobile policies, your home policy, and an umbrella policy.

I offered all my clients, making over $100K per year, long-term care insurance. Usually, they had health and life insurance. Even multi-millionaires struggled with paying for the cost of long-term care insurance. But the cost is real.

I have had to put my mother in elder care after knee surgery, as she needed help to get to the bathroom and help in the bathroom. Our family quickly spent $125,000 on elder care and $100,000 on knee surgeries. Our insurance covered the surgeries, but we paid for the elder care out of pocket.

Few people think they will need elder care or that their parent's care could significantly impact their own retirement plans because they need to help fund their elder care expenses.

Additionally, only some of my clients had adequate life insurance, usually because their company paid for it. You need to own life insurance for wage earners and homemakers, in case they die prematurely, so that living expenses, care for children, children's education, and other financial goals, such as retirement, can be funded, regardless. Premature death is a risk that many clients do not prepare for, or do not prepare for adequately with life insurance.

Chapter Seven

HOW TO MINIMIZE TAXES

One of your most important jobs as an investor is to earn investment returns and minimize taxes. So we will discuss different types of investment accounts where you can accumulate money to meet your financial goals, and minimize the. taxes on these accounts.

One of the best things you can do to accumulate money to invest is to save in your company's 401K plan. Remember that this money is not taxed when you make it on your or your company's contributions. It is taxed when you take cash out. I mention this as many retirement plans estimate current income tax rates between 25% and 35%, likely much lower than the rates you will pay when you take money out. Rollover IRAs or regular IRAs are taxes just like your 401k funds. You don't pay taxes when you invest in the account, but it is taxable at the current rates when you take money out. So the first two types of investment accounts you can invest in are 401K plans and IRAs, and both have the same taxes; you pay income tax on the distributions when you take money out.

A good alternative or additional way to save money for your financial goals is to invest in a Roth IRA. Roth IRAs are the third investment account you can open to save money for your long-term financial goals. It would be best to do this in addition to saving and investing in your company's 401k plan. You will pay taxes on the income you invest in the Roth IRA. But since you paid taxes on the ROTH IRA contributions up front, you do not pay income taxes when you take distributions from those funds. Think of the ROTH. IRA like this: you have tax risk on the 401K and Rollover IRAs, and taxes will be higher when you take money out. You are reducing your tax risk with the ROTH IRA because you already paid taxes on the income before you invested in the ROTH.

So, please, take advantage of the ability to save more in a ROTH IRA. You can make up to $153,000 annually [modified adjusted gross income] for 2023 and $161,000 [MAGI] for 2024, and save $6,500 [age 49 or below] or $7,500 if you are over 50 for 2023, and $7,000 [age 49 or below] or $8,000 if you are over 50.

The fourth way to save for financial goals through investing is through a taxable investment account. A taxable investment account means paying taxes like funding a ROTH IRA. But the good thing is that you only pay taxes only on the gains. So, if you hold a stock for a year and one day, you lower the taxes by having a long-term capital gain and a long-term capital gains rate, of 0% to 20% in 2023, based upon your taxable income bracket and tax filing status, likely lower than your income tax rate. You control when you sell: if you can hold your positions for a year or more, you have reduced your taxes, and overall tax risk.

Why should you invest in your company 401K, a ROTH IRA, and a taxable investment account? So you can diversify your tax risk. Think of your investment for your long-term financial goals like this: let's say you have, at retirement, $2,000,000 in an IRA, with the income distributions taken out of this fund taxable at 40%, and you have $2,000,000 in a ROTH IRA. Which will provide more for your financial and retirement goals?

The ROTH will give you far more money than the taxable IRA, which you likely rolled over from your company 401K plan because of the income taxes paid to the IRS on regular IRA deductions. The ROTH will have no taxes on the distributions as you already paid taxes when you contributed each year to the ROTH. The IRA will have $800,000 or more in tax when you take money out, and the ROTH will have zero taxes when you take cash out. Which would you prefer? The ROTH will provide much higher distributions, because of the taxes were already paid. There is no tax on distributions from a ROTH IRA.

Sadly, most clients and investors do not think about the tax consequences of their investing. They believe that their investment $$$ are equal whether they go into a 401K, IRA, IRA rollover account, ROTH, taxable Investment account, or a whole life insurance policy. They are not. Long-term investment in ROTH IRAs, whole-life insurance, and taxable investment accounts is all superior to 401K and IRAs.

You should invest in all of them. And when you have to choose between them, choose the more tax-efficient investment vehicles [structures], such as the ROTH IRA, whole life insurance, and taxable investment accounts. They will net you more money after tax. What is most important is the money you have after tax. You cannot spend income that pays taxes to the government.

Another way to minimize your taxes in investing is to buy municipal bonds because the income is tax-free. The tax-free nature of municipal bonds is the US government's way of encouraging you to invest in these bonds. Ensure you invest in investment-grade municipalities [cities] with experts helping you select and buy these bonds. A good place to invest in municipal bonds if your taxable investment account.

At Merrill Lynch, I had bond experts on speed dial, and if I needed a 1-5 year duration, or 5-10 year duration, or 11-30 year duration, meaning the life maturityof the bonds, they would design portfolios to match, and they did an outstanding job in every case. I bought several million dollars of bonds from the Merrill Lynch bond desk.

How can you save money on your taxes?

1. **Make full use of your company's 401K plan and the company match**. For 2023, you can contribute up to $22,500 [if you are under age 50] and $30,000 [before tax] if you are over 50. You can contribute $66,000 to company plans, the balance being contributions after-tax [after you have contributed either. Up to $22,500 or $30,000 pre-tax]. If you are able, then make the after-tax contributions, and lower the tax risk [the risk that income taxes go up when you withdraw your investment assets from an IRA]. In 2024, you can contribute up to $23,000 to your 401k plan.

2. **Make sure you utilize a CPA** if your income is $150,000 or more as a single person and your family income is over $200,000 if you are married. A CPA can save money on taxes, and advise you specifically on your financial and investment plan.

3. **Eliminate all mutual fund investments** unless they are the only options to invest in your company's 401k plan. Mutual funds are the most fee-heavy, backwards, dinosaur investment you can make, that carries an excessive management fees. If you can invest in ETFs, do that because they are more tax-efficient vehicles with lower management fees. Also, individual stock positions [such as BP, XOM, etc. and ETFs are more tax efficient because you can hold them and pay capital gains taxes by having them for one year [and a day].

4. **Most mutual funds can be replicated** [replaced] by ETFs [Exchange trade funds, say, that hold the S&P500 stocks, for example, or small-cap or mid-cap stocks. Their management fees are lower, putting more money in your pockets.

5. **Make sure you are taking advantage of all tax deductions available to you**. 179 deductions are deductions the IRS allows a business owner to deduct up to $ 1.080 million for 2023 and $1.16

million in 2024, for investment in equipment, such as computers and machinery. The 179 deduction is fantastic for business owners investing in their businesses.

My Advice:

1. **My clients did most of their savings in 401k's and Rollover IRAs and thus faced significant tax risk if and when income tax rates rose.** Tax risks are the number one reason why retirement plans fail. The Number two reason for failure of retirement plans is poor management of investments and investment risks, [not getting out of equities when equities are declining 20% or more, taking those losses, which is dumb].

2. **I did my best to encourage clients who did most of their savings in 401ks and rollover IRAs to invest in ROTH IRAs and whole-life insurance**, where they could minimize taxes within the ROTH IRA and whole-life policy and thus diversity their tax risk. This issue of future income taxes is crucial for clients and must be understood better and more completely by advisors and clients. Think about what is better: isn't it better to have paid the income taxes now and not have tax surprises later? Again, most clients think more money is better now.

3. **Most clients are deceived by their investment portfolios invested in tax-inefficient vehicles like 401ks, IRAs, and Rollover IRAs**. The government owns a significant share of these investments. If income taxes are 50% when you retire, the US government will own half of your 401K, IRA, and Rollover IRA. It hurts to think this way, but this is reality.

4. **When investing in a taxable investment account, carefully select your stocks**. You want to hold them long enough to earn long-term capital gains and then pay lower taxes on your profits. You

must own stocks, ETFs, or bonds for one year or more to qualify for long-term capital gains. So less volatile investments make more sense here: think oil stocks, and be happy for dividend income. More volatile investments such as international stocks and small cap stocks do not fit here: I would put stops on all equities, and volatile ones, when they stop out [sell] would likely cause income taxes instead of capital gains. A taxable investment account is the best place to hold municipal bonds because you get no tax benefits inside an IRA but do in a taxable investment account, as the income from bonds investments is tax-free. Depending upon your holding period [needs to be one year and one day for capital gains], you will have a capital gain or loss on all bond investments.

5. **Maximum fund a ROTH IRA**. You are saving money on taxes for the long term. Most clients do not value this ability and do not take advantage of it, in my experience.

6. **Maximum fund whole life insurance policies on all wage-earners, and policies for your children, if you can.** When you look at the risks of investing and recognize all the costs of investing, in terms of investment expenses, risk of loss, losses, inflation, and taxes, the returns inside a whole life policy look excellent, due to lower risk. And when an insurance company pays out a life insurance claim, the heirs inherit that tax-free. The tax-free nature of life insurance makes the returns from life insurance equal [can be higher] than investments based on risk and more excellent than investments if large payouts from whole life insurance policies are distributed to heirs. I would argue returns on a life insurance policy, started when you are young, are higher per unit of risk than 95% of investments in equities. The higher return argument for equities is just the fuel advisory firms and advisors use to get you to take more risk. Many investors, especially 60 years old and above, and retirees, should be taking less risk, not more.

7. **Maximize your charitable deductions**. You can utilize donor-advised funds or set up your 501C. Consider giving appreciated stock(s) to charities.

Storytime

Only a few of my clients would allow me access to their investments, insurance, retirement & financial plans, estate plan, etc. All of them let me access their investments. I did my best for all of them.

But I could only make investments based on what clients shared with me.

I did my best work when clients allowed me access to all their financial plans, including estate plans, retirement plans, and insurance. Then I could comprehend the risks to their financial plan against a broader perspective for their financial plans, what they wanted to achieve.

For example, when I knew a client wanted $150,000 per year income for their retirement plan, and they wanted to give their kids $1,000,000 each in cash, plus their remaining assets, and if I knew their estate plan, I could gain a comprehensive understanding of risk across all their financial goals, and know more appropriately how to invest.

For clients that shared all their financial plans with me, including taxes, estate plans, financial plans, and insurance, I could get more insurance coverage for the same money and reduce risk. And for those that shared their tax returns with me, I could decrease investment expenses, increase deductions, and lower taxes. I relied on CPAs to prepare tax returns and advice and referred clients to CPAs. [CPAs were very poor at referring clients to me, but I forgive them].

My review of tax returns primarily resulted in getting rid of mutual funds expenses [outside of 401K funds], itemizing more deductible expenses, such as investment expenses [publications, fees on their investment accounts] by clarifying more items that were deductible, encouraging 179 deductions for equipment if they owned a business, and charitable deductions [giving stock or appreciated assets to charities; this at times, became part of an estate plan].

The **bottom line** is that I helped clients reduce expenses, allowed them to invest more, and got closer to their financial goals by reducing taxes. I found that good CPAs can save clients hundreds of thousands of dollars over time after their fees by lowering taxes and assisting clients in reducing taxes on income and the sale of assets.

Chapter Eight
Retirement Planning

Most of my clients during my career were people whose primary financial goal was a secure retirement. So we will discuss retirement planning, recent trends, what makes for a sound retirement plan, shortfalls in planning, some advice, and some stories.

What are the current trends in retirement planning?

1. **Healthcare costs are increasing, affecting** the cost of disability, health, and long-term care insurance.

2. **Asset allocation and risk management** are the most important during the ten years before retirement. A 60% stock and 40% bond allocation are the most common.

3. **Adequate emergency funds and health and long-term care insurance** are vital to keeping the plan on track. If funds must be withdrawn to meet health or other cash needs, the retirement plan is at risk of failure.[29]

---

[29] Barron's, article "The 10 years before Retirement are Critical, How to be Ready," by Elizabeth O'Brien.

Health insurers are seeking premiums to rise 10-20% this year [which must be approved by state governments],[30]

It isn't only health insurance costs from private insurers that are rising. Medicare Part B premium costs are expected to increase also, estimated to grow "6.3% in 2024, 6.2% in 2025, 8% in 2026, 7.8% in 2027, and around 6% annually through 2031.[31]

Another trend is for retirement investing is target-based funds, which are designed to meet the asset allocation goals of a particular maturity, say ten years from now, for clients who plan to retire in the next ten years. These funds are expected to more closely match the asset allocation needed for the retiree and usually have a 60% stock and 40% bond allocation to avoid taking too much risk and incurring losses.

What are some old retirement planning trends going by the wayside?

1. **Simple rules of thumb**, **estimating distributions** to be 4% or 5% of the retirement funds accumulated. For example, in a $2 million portfolio, a client takes $100,000 per year. Per this quick and dirty calculation, the funds will last twenty years. No one assumes this anymore.

2. **Rates of return on investment cannot be a simple arithmetic average** like that used in most Monte Carlo analyses. From 2009 to 2021, the S&P 500 averaged 16% annualized returns for these thirteen years. But in 2022, the S&P 500 fell 20%, and bonds, tracked

---

[30] McKinsey & Company article, "Sharp Healthcare Inflation through 2027, McKinsey Website, Google search dated February 15, 2023.
[31] Barron's article, Barron's website, "Retirees: Expect to Get Hit with Surging Health Costs", by Gail Marks Jarvis, dated 3.20.23, accessed 3.27.23.

by US Aggregate Bond Index exchange fund ticker AGG, dropped 13%.[32] [quote O'brien article, above].

3. **Over-simplified Monte Carlo analysis of arithmetic rates of return for retirement planning**. These "retirement plans" waste effort since they do not capture actual data. I prefer to use current rates of return for the S&P 500 for plans, and then project that for five years, and raise tax rates to 40% to see if the plan fails. If it does, it needs more work and planning.

What is a sound retirement plan? First, it has both an accumulation plan and a distribution plan. Second, it is a plan that has reasonable assumptions about the future. Remember when I talked about financial goals? Financial plans always have assumptions about: the **income tax rate** you expect for the income & investment income you take as a distribution when you retire or desire money from your investments is **critical.** I suggest using 35% or more and gradually increasing that over the next five to ten years.

What is an accumulation plan?
It is the plan that has estimates of investment return, inflation, and future tax rates and uses your current investment portfolio balance to project when you would reach your savings goal for retiring. **Remember that all but your investment balance is a projection based on a long-term average.**

Thus, an accumulation plan is primarily a way to answer the question: when do I have enough money to retire? **An accumulation plan answers your most important questions: "how much do I need to retire?"**

---

[32] Barron's, article "The 10 years before Retirement are Critical, How to be Ready," by Elizabeth O'Brien.

[your retirement savings goal] and "how much can I earn off my investments", which meets your income goal for retiring.

Any advisor can project a rate of return of 12%; however, only the best advisors can consistently deliver above average returns. Most advisors underestimate the rate of inflation. In 2022 in the US, inflation was at least 9%; for many cost of living items, the highest inflation rate in forty years for consumer goods. And, most advisors underestimate future income tax rates when you take money out.

Most advisors have a Monte Carlo analysis software program that runs probability scenarios, the % chance you have of achieving your financial goal. It will run and test your retirement under various assumptions, say 10,000 to 100,000 times. Using Monte Carlo analysis, you can confidently know that your plan has a 90% chance of success. Are you comfortable with a plan with only a 90% chance of achievement? You can run plans that say they have a 95% chance of accomplishment, yet these plans use historical averages. How will your retirement plan work with higher inflation, taxes, and possibly lower investment returns? I see little value in Monte Carlo analysis.

Although most advisory firms use Monte Carlo analysis as a quick and dirty way to say they did retirement planning, Monte Carlo analysis has serious shortcomings. First, it is limited to a probability analysis. No client wants to think they only have an 85% or 90% of meeting their retirement goals. Second, it is determined by the number of simulations run, usually 10,000. I would run 100,000 or 1 million or more Monte Carlo simulations and learn how many simulations where the plan's success fails.

Third, Monte Carlo simulations significantly underestimate catastrophic events, such as bear markets, recessions, or any other financial crisis that can impact the value of your investment portfolio. For example, if you have significant bond investments equal to $1 million or more of your portfolio, you have had lower than average long-term bond returns, significantly below the 5% to 6% average income bonds have produced historically. Let's say this affects you for five years, and you earned 2% instead of 5%. You lost 3% per year for five years on $1 million, a loss of $150,000 in income. How do you make that up? How do you make up for two or more equity market crashes where you had a year of losses and a few short years to make that up? What results do you need now to make up for years of losses? Every investor needs more time to make up for years of losses.

What is a retirement distribution plan?

A retirement distribution plan is a cash flow plan that assumes specific rates of return on investments, along with income tax rates and rates of inflation, to determine that the plan is reasonable. It is another test to ensure the client's investment portfolio and assets are sufficient to meet their retirement plan financial goal. The plan has outputs of five to ten years of cash flow to ensure the retirement program works. Usually, the goal of a distribution plan is to verify that the client has a certain amount of money after-tax.

Most retirement plans consist only of a simple accumulation plan analyzed with Monte Carlo simulations. Most retirement plans do not have distribution plans. And most clients need to have their investment portfolios reviewed monthly or quarterly so the investment assets will achieve the rate of return as required by the retirement plan. If retirement investment assets are not reviewed as often as necessary, this casts serious doubt whether retirement plan goals can be achieved. If the advisor does not make monthly and quarterly changes to the portfolio, then I am concerned that the plan will not be achieved due to poor management of investment assets.

Current trends in retirement planning include more emphasis on contemporary lifestyle and not just accumulation, thus more balance between pure saving and investing. Additionally, there is more emphasis now on what can break or seriously disrupt retirement plans. One example is ensuring that health and long-term care insurance avoid depleting investment assets from client health issues. Another example would be more income planning during equity market downturns to reduce investment risk, prevent losses in equities, and distribute funds saved for retirement. A final example would be assisting clients by clarifying their understanding of what they can expect from Social Security, Medicare, and insurance.

My Advice:

1. **Most advisors will underestimate the inflation rates and future tax rates**. Remember that both inflation and future tax rates are average. You have to adjust both rates for spikes, and there will likely be large up spikes of both in the next five to ten years.

2. **Most advisors overestimate the rate of return and do not adjust your plan when they incur losses**. And any investment losses are always someone else's fault, not theirs. Keep your advisor accountable. If they have losses for your investment portfolio two years in a row, get a new investment advisor. They don't know what they are doing. And likely, they are not using risk management tools like 5% stops on equity positions. [By the way, you can also use stops in bonds, say 3% stop, meaning a sell order if you drop 3% in value].

3. **Investment returns are also averages.** If you have lost money in the last year or two, consider what return you need to compensate for those losses to keep your financial plan on track. And is that investment return reasonable? Any advisor can promise high returns, but that usually comes at the cost of riskier investments. And if they lose money again, you are left with 30% losses to make up in the long term to keep your financial plan.

4. **Most advisors should create a retirement distribution plan, five years before you retire, to project cash flows from your expected investment account values.** And advisors need to update the retirement accumulation plan after equity markets have fallen or if the client has to make more than regular withdrawals from their investment accounts.

5. **Advisors should review your investment portfolios monthly or quarterly and make changes to the asset allocation.** I needed to consistently move money to different sectors during the US business cycle, to improve the performance, and take gains on equities and ETFs that had already peaked.

6. **Most of my clients assumed a zero return from Social Security.** Some will receive benefits. But these benefits take time to forecast. It de[ends upon a client's income during retirement as to whether they will receive Social Security. If you earn more that $22,320 in 2024, you will not have any Social Security benefit. So, Social Security is only a backstop for lower income clients.

7. **I'm afraid I disagree with having a large portion of client assets in target-based funds to reach retirement goals.** The advisor can do this for the client and save investing costs for these glorified asset allocations, from higher expense mutual funds. If your advisor cannot make these same allocations at a lower fee, then find another advisor .

8. **What is more important than the target-based funds** is choosing whether to be in the market. If there are sell signals, such as 20% spikes in the $VIX, bank failures, or small-, mid-, and large-cap stocks [using tickers IWM, MDY, and SPY] all breaking their 50-day, and 200-day moving averages downward, then the client should be out of equities, and out of all asset allocation funds. If there are no sell signals, and IWM, MDY, and SPY are all moving up above

50-day and 200-day lines, with no spikes in volatility, the client should be at least 60% stocks and 40% bonds. I would consider having moderate investors at 70% stocks and 30% bonds due to the lower investing risk at this time when equity markets are rising.

9. **I suggest a more rigorous, retirement plan analysis in the five years before retirement than is usually performed.** It should analyze the following: what are the plan's successes in the past five years? [in terms of returns, minimizing losses, gains in wealth or funds for retirement, increased savings and lower taxes, etc.] What are the risks to the achievement of the retirement plan goals[should include discussion of investment returns by current managers, inflation, taxes, US economy, changes to retirement plan age, accountability of current advisor, and performance of current investment managers. Based on the successes and the risks, what should be done now to achieve the retirement plan goals? Who is doing that? I don't know of any advisory firm that addresses retirement planning with the scrutiny and depth in financial planning that it deserves, outlined here.

10. **Retirement plans must include a distribution plan.** I suggest using the client's real rates of return for the past five years and projecting cash flows based on that. If the plan fails, then make changes. This may require higher savings, cutting household expenses, or tweaking the asset allocation. It may mean finding a better advisor, who can avoid losses, and who can do the meaningful investment management and retirement planning that you need.

Storytime
Only about 20% of my clients wanted to talk specifically about retirement planning. Some were too wealthy to have those discussions.

For those who wanted to discuss retirement planning, we would talk about their income goal for retirement after tax, and I would estimate some rates of return and income tax rates to determine when they would achieve their goal. My clients expected me to achieve the rate of return on investments. But the tax rate estimate for their future income distributions was always an estimate, like throwing darts.

Most of my retirement planning clients needed clarification that the future income tax rate was an estimate and that those rates could be much higher. We both agreed that we wanted those tax rates to be as low as possible. But do not always get what we want.

I had a client for retirement planning, making $400,000 per year and saving $250,000 per year for retirement. He also wanted to give each of his four children one million each. We built a retirement plan, added some life insurance, did an annuity as he wanted to retire soon, that would provide guarantees that his income would be a certain amount. I did some of my best work in investing, insurance, and financial planning for this client.

He quit his job, cut household expenses, and broke everything I built. He cut the insurance policy, saying he could not pay for that without his $400,000 per year job. He decided to substantially reduce what he wanted to give to his children. He canceled the annuity as he said he could figure out how to guarantee his income without paying for insurance on his investments. He broke the whole financial plan. He wanted to be a strategist. This was heartbreaking to me. But I had to fire this client. I cannot work with clients who do not follow any of my advice.

He was the client that every advisor thinks is attractive [with his income and assets of about $5 million] but was not. In spite of my efforts, he was not happy. But I didn't quit that job for him. I invested based on what he told me were his goals. I bought the annuity because he was telling me he was about to retire. No one needs clients like this. Bottom line:

he was a consultant strategist and wanted to be a strategist even though he was not competent to be a his own financial strategist. I wish him the best. I doubt his plan is working as he hoped.

Chapter Nine

FINANCIAL PLANNING & ESTATE PLANNING

This chapter discusses the importance of financial planning in achieving specific financial goals, and why estate planning is crucial to transferring your wealth to family or charities.

So, what do financial plans accomplish? They can tell me how much and how long it takes to achieve your financial goal or goals. For example, if you want to retire with $100,000 per year and make certain assumptions about taxes and investment rates of return, say 5% return and 25% tax, you need $2 million to retire and receive income for 20 years and have $75,000 after taxes.

Most of the financial planning I performed was assisting clients in knowing what they needed to retire and how long they money would last under various assumptions. I usually encourage clients to save more and understand that if income taxes went up and investment returns went down, what that would do to their plan.

What are some other reasons to do financial planning? Some clients want to give large amounts to family members. Others wish to plan their retirement out of a family-owned business. Sometimes you have family members as employees of a family business, and the family prepares for them to take over the family-owned company. In contrast, other family members will receive an inheritance but not management or control of a business. Trying to get fairness between family members who inherit and others who run businesses takes time and effort. Here the lines blur between financial and estate planning, as both are involved in this scenario.

So, financial plans assist clients in knowing how long and when they can meet their goals, such as retirement, overall savings, and investment goals, and specifically, what goals are realistic and which are not.

When should you update your overall financial plan? When you have changes in employment, income, assets, or when your financial goals or timelines have changed.

Now we will discuss estate planning. Both insurance and financial planning contribute to estate planning.

What is estate planning? It is arranging your legal, personal, and financial matters so that when you die, your family and/or charities will receive your assets and be able to use them.

The first step in estate planning is to have a will or trust. You should talk to an estate planning attorney. I recommend getting referrals for them from CPAs or other financial professionals. You might find lists of estate planning attorneys in your local business journal. If you are married, you each get a will or trust based on the advice of your attorney.

What will a will or trust do for you?

It will list your assets, such as land, investments, businesses, equipment, etc., and who you want to receive them upon your death. Some assets, such as bank and investment accounts, legally pass by law, by whom you name as the beneficiary or beneficiary. Your attorney will ask you: What do you want to happen when you die? To whom will you distribute your assets?

A will states what assets you own and determines who will receive them. One negative about wills is that they are public documents that anyone can access. If you want privacy in what you own and how they are distributed, you most likely want a trust.

There are a variety of trusts. An AB trust is designed to maximize estate tax deductions and creates a trust for each spouse to gain those deductions. Living trusts are flexible and can be used to gather assets into one place and maintain privacy. Living trusts can become irrevocable to gain tax benefits and asset protection. The only downfall here is that an irrevocable trust cannot be changed, and thus there needs to be more flexibility in administering the trust. A QTIP trust [Qualified Terminal Interest Property] provides for a spouse's income while another person inherits the property. You will have to discuss these options with your attorney. Let them recommend the structures [type of trust] they recommend for you. You do not need to be an expert in trusts, just know the type of trust your attorney utilizes for you and your family.

Some tough decisions in this estate planning process can be the following:

Dividing assets among children, some of whom work in a family business and some who do not. Most commonly, the children working in the family-owned company inherit the corporation's stock. Life insurance will be purchased [on the owner of this business, either one or both spouses] to provide the inheritance for children not working in the family business [doing your best to equalize the children's inheritances].

You are deciding how children inherit your assets, possibly, from different marriages or those of husband and wife, with equal or unequal shares. Also, in the case of adopted children, they may or may not inherit equally with the other children.

Why do estate planning?

If a person dies without a will or trust, they die intestate, and the state's laws where they died or lived will determine how assets will split among heirs. For example, most state laws have parents and uncles inheriting portfolios for an unmarried person who dies. This asset distribution likely differs from how the person who recently passed would want the assets distributed.

The bottom line is that you plan your estate so the people you want to inherit your assets get your assets.

How is estate planning done?

Usually, estate planning is done with an attorney, with the involvement of financial advisors and CPAs. The primary documents are legal, creating a will or trust for married spouses or singles. Financial advisors need to know the plan, specifically how the beneficiaries should be named on investment accounts, so the investment account beneficiaries are the same as the trust or will, to represent the wishes of the will or trust.

A will meets state laws and reveals the person's intentions to distribute their assets and pay their bills upon death. A trust can be living or irrevocable; living trusts hold a person's assets while they live. The irrevocable trust manages assets after their death and continues operating them after death. There are several varieties of trusts. What is important is that you have a will or trust by a reputable attorney.

Common shortfalls in estate planning:

1. **While the wills or trust documents are created,** the financial advisor or bank does not change the beneficiaries to reflect what the will or trust says. In other words, the beneficiaries of the insurance and investment accounts must be updated according to the attorney's specifications in the trust agreement or will. And then, the beneficiaries stated on the account will determine the distribution of assets, not the intent of the person creating the will or trust.

2. **Businesses that have values that fluctuate**, such as private, family-owned companies, real estate, or oil-producing properties, and

families may not get annual valuations to update the value of the business[s], either up or down. Then, the splits among heirs are not equal or as intended, which may lead to lawsuits.

3. **Wills or trust agreements may not be updated after they are created.** Sometimes, based on relationships, someone is cut out of the will or not cut out of the determination or guidance of the testator [person making the will] or trust creator [whose assets will be managed or distributed]. And insurance policies may lapse or not be updated.

4. **Some businesses are unusual, and it is difficult to determine their value.** There are business valuation experts, but a similar business must exist to determine a fair valuation. Otherwise, it is a big guess and may be unfair to heirs.

Insurance and financial planning are usually closely interrelated with estate planning. Insurance would be specified and given to certain heirs who inherit upon a person's passing. And financial planning is likely to be involved in determining the value of a business or investments and dividing them among heirs.

My Advice

1. **Most retirement plans need more detail because these plans are accumulation plans only, not distribution plans.** That plans says when the client will have a certain amount of money but does not describe how this retirement plan will work when the client is taking distributions. And most of these plans do not adjust or assume higher taxes or lower investment rates in the future. You may have a projection with a high probability of success, but this plan may fail due to higher taxes, lower investment returns, and investment returns that are realistic.

2. **When a client was ready to retire, I would perform a distribution analysis**. I would schedule five years of distributions from the portfolio under various investment returns and income taxes to establish their investment portfolios were sufficient to accomplish their financial goals. That is always better than a Monte Carlo analysis.

3. **Some clients wanted to be the financial strategist** and thought it was a weakness to reveal information about their families and estate planning goals . When I knew each client's goals [if they would tell me], I could do a better job of investing and more appropriately take the risk [but not too much trouble] to achieve their overall financial goals. But transparency and trust is not easy to create.

4. **Some clients have the "smartest person alive syndrome."** They assume only they are smart, and no one can advise them. I could not work with these clients; they wanted to run with their investment and planning ideas. I found that I could not work with such clients and I promptly fired them.

5. **I offered some clients non-traditional advice** about accumulating their retirement goals. It depended on the client whether they were able to process that advice. For example, you can earn and gain investment returns in 401K or IRAs, but you will take distributions later at a likely higher income tax rate. Those later income tax rates could be higher due to national deficits, inflation, and possibly lower investment returns. Investing in other savings structures, such as ROTH IRAs or taxable investment accounts, or even whole life insurance, is wise as you lower the risk of higher taxes.

6. **Most clients need to realize how much taxes affect their accumulation plans.** It is much easier to accumulate money and achieve an overall retirement funding goal than to get 5% from the portfolio over 20 years. The distribution part is the hardest, and

most advisors do zero planning for the distribution element of a retirement plan.

7. **Ensure you have a financial planner to do the complex planning you need.** Some financial planners work with people getting divorced and can separate assets into buckets for these parties. If you are doing retirement planning, make sure your advisor is not just an investment person but someone who takes your retirement goals seriously and facilitates your planning and investment goals.

Storytime

Most of my clients already had trusts or wills for estate planning, especially among families with generational wealth being passed over the past two or three generations.

I remember assisting two 60-year-old married clients with $3 million in assets in estate planning. I helped them hire an attorney who created trusts for the clients based on their wishes. They owned businesses and retained investments in several firms from consulting, so they needed a continuing structure to manage their assets. This client also had adopted children, and this family had different inheritances for each child. It was complex. And the client changed his mind about what each would inherit almost annually.

One thing struck me. I studied all the various legal forms of wills and trusts. Most people with money took the more complex legal route, primarily trusts, primarily to keep the transfer of wealth in their family confidential.

A **good choice for many people is to have a living trust that holds assets; upon death, it turns into an irrevocable trust.** A living trust is flexible and can be changed at any time. A living trust that becomes an irrevocable trust is suitable for gathering assets into one place [not leaving unnamed assets behind, and usually using legal language that states all assets of Mr. or Mrs. XXX become a part of the irrevocable trust] and controlling the assets. That is good if your estate plan needs a legal and management structure. It helps if the irrevocable trust holds flexible assets like cash, insurance policies, and investment accounts.

But the irrevocable trust makes it more challenging to manage when there are multiple beneficiaries with different needs. The irrevocable trust is going to control the assets and never give up control. For example, one child may run a business and will gain control [with ownership of the LLC or Corporation] and inherit it. Another child may inherit a house and money. Another child may need financing to start a business. The irrevocable trust can deal with these different needs, but dividing the assets can be more complex, and the trust [the management structure for these different assets] is trying to control assets when inheritors want to manage and control them. The trust is most likely to retain control in this situation.

A key point is whether a legal structure should be in place after death to control assets. Is that helpful? Sometimes the legal structure that is good for estate administration could be more beneficial to heirs who want to receive and control those assets. The Irrevocable trust would be suitable where the children, or inheritors, need management and are not given control [say one is mentally ill, has a criminal past, or does not have the business background to run the family business], etc.

Additionally, the problem heirs have with most irrevocable trusts is that they cannot change. Some tax benefits and asset protection behind irrevocable trusts are highly beneficial. You will need to discuss your plans to distribute your assets one day with a qualified attorney.

Most people think they have time to do estate planning later. It is much better to have a plan, face your mortality, and leave a clear plan to your family. What is difficult for many families, after the death of a parent, is trying to figure out what they wanted, if they left no plan. And children and spouses may have vastly different ideas of what the deceased wanted for their family. You can minimize strife in your family by leaving clear direction about how you want your assets distributed, and how any businesses should be managed.

Chapter Ten

CONCLUDING THOUGHTS

We have covered many topics, including advisory firms and advisors, investments, investment reports, life insurance, long-term care insurance, disability insurance, and health insurance. And we have discussed financial planning, estate planning, and retirement planning. I also offer some explanation of risk, as I see it, advice on fees and when investments are timely, achieving your financial goals, and finally, when you should move assets.

Now I will offer my concluding thoughts. If I have repeated advice, then I consider it crucial and worth repeating.

What issues are most important in building wealth?
Which topics are most important regarding investments, insurance, and financial planning? In my experience, most clients outweigh the value of building their investment assets, giving insurance and financial planning too little time and money. Insurance can eliminate catastrophic damage to a persons or famlies' wealth.

That is why I recommend your deal with your insurance risks first. If you have not addressed these risks, you are not ready to take on the additional investment risks. Many clients want to invest first, even in falling equity markets. If equities are falling and interest rates are rising. It would be best to save the money in cash and wait to invest until interest rates have peaked and equities are rising again. Deal with insurance risks that can be catastrophic to your wealth building.

And if equity markets are falling, do financial planning for your primary lifetime financial goals? Insurance companies and their advisors will handle this assignment best. They are superior financial planners, better than most investment advisors, and know insurance products well.

Then when you start working on investments, you have reduced as much risk as possible on the insurance side. And carry those risk-management strategies with you: does your Advisor use risk management tools such as 5% stops? Use options? If not, find an advisor who does use these risk-management strategies. It could save you time and money, $500,000 or $1 million, or more.

Most clients should hire advisors to manage their money. The only exception would be if you are a financial advisor, have significant investment training, and have an excellent five to ten-year record of managing money with above-average results, beating the S&P 500 index for any year 95% of the time. Most people need to be better investors. Many advisors need to be more accountable for their results. Many aspire to be great investors, but most require the intelligence, drive, discipline, or work ethic to bring that to pass. A good investor needs to read at least one to two hours daily.

I recommend that you read the book **Crucial Accountability**. Most of us need to learn how to hold others accountable and have accountability discussions. Is your Advisor responsible and accountable for your investment results? Are they meeting your investing goals, your financial goals? At times, they are not. Are you ready to hold them accountable? I encourage you to learn how to have these conversations with your Advisor.

If you have had an Advisor for several years and have yet to have specific portfolio and performance reviews, start having them now. Have your Advisor discuss their performance each quarter and every year. How does that performance compare to the S&P 500? Or with another appropriate index?

What is Risk?

Risk is the probability of loss. Suppose you are investing when the volatility index has spiked 20% above its average 50-day line. In that case, large banks are going broke, and IWM, MDY, and SPY indexes [small-, mid-, and large cap stocks] are breaking their 50-day and 200-day moving averages, so you have a high probability of loss. When this is happening, It is time to get out of equity markets.

Another reason you should get out of equities when these sell indicators exist [above paragraph concerning volatility and market indexes, banking] is that too much money speculating in markets exacerbates market swings. It causes the money flows into and out of equity positions to be larger and have a more significant effect.

Risk is complex and challenging to grasp.

That is because there are **layers of risk** we need to maintain awareness of. To me, the primary risk layers are:

1. US economy, GDP growth, debt, inflation, and taxes

2. International economies, GDP growth, debt, inflation, and taxes

3. Money supply growth for each economy where you have invested, especially the US. Excessive growth in printed money leads to inflation, as does excessive national debt.

4. The overall health of the US and international banking sector

5. The volatility of equity and bond markets in the US, Europe, & Asia

6. Performance of major indexes, IWM, MDY, and SPY in the US

7. Performance of significant indexes abroad, where you invest, by country or by capitalization [small, mid, large-capitalization]

8. Company risk that varies for each stock and bond position that you own

9. Portfolio Manager risk that they make money, not lose money, in current market conditions [which change]

10. Advisor Firm risk: that they support their Advisors, and do not make onerous demands, that compliance is reasonable for Advisors.

11. Advisor risk, their accountability, performance, knowledge, biases, and awareness to make changes when plans do not work

12. Client risk: are they stable? do their financial plans change monthly? Is the client taking too many distributions and destroying wealth?.

These are the critical layers of risk. Risk is far more than what is happening in equity and bond markets. A good project for a finance doctoral student would be to develop a comprehensive measure of risk that addresses these twelve items. That would be groundbreaking. And likely, they would think of other areas of risk that have never been quantified or explored. [Just thinking outside the box: products used by Advisors, if inappropriate, present another layer of risk].

Due to these multiple layers of risk [twelve items, the first bundle of risk, referred to as economic, market, firm, Advisor, and performance risks], **Advisor awareness of these risks requires a great amount of discipline to be successful**. Unless the Advisor is held accountable, the risk management quickly breaks down. Holding the portfolio manager and the Advisor responsible is critical to fulfilling a client's financial goals. If both the portfolio manager and Advisor are doing their jobs, then financial goals can be achieved; with this, with goals such as retirement, are more likely to succeed.

Additionally, there is a risk in financial planning of being comprehensive in all the areas of financial planning: investments, insurance, estate planning, retirement planning, etc. These risks are the second bundle of risk I call planning risk. What is missing in financial planning is a comprehensive measure of risk across all the essential planning areas, not just investments, but including insurance, tax risk, estate plan risk of failure, retirement plan failure, etc. How well has the Advisor and client addressed Investments? Insurance? Estate Planning? Retirement Planning? This is never done at the 100% level. I urge you to do your best to accomplish that.

For example, how can we quantify the risk that the Retirement plan will not be fulfilled beyond simple arithmetic returns [and simplistic Monte Carlo analysis], using the client's real return data for the past five to ten years? How much of this risk falls on the Advisor for their product and money manager choices within investments? For getting out of equities when equities fall 10-20% annually? Or concerning their accountability for the retirement plan to make changes when it is not working? How much of the risk for the retirement plan's potential failure is on the client for failing to save more and expecting too much of their investments and the advisor?

Thirdly, there is a risk that Advisors may not be adequately trained in all areas of financial planning. These risks are the third major bundle of risk: education, training, and experience risk. It may have changed, but Merrill Lynch was outstanding in training in investments, a bit behind the bar in training on insurance and financial planning. Their estate planning was more than adequate. And Guardian Life Insurance was phenomenal on disability, long-term care, and life insurance and excellent on financial planning. But at the time I trained, it was inferior in Investments. I was already trained in investments by Merrill Lynch and did not need that training. However, most Advisors I met there wanted to make money selling investment products but needed to improve in their knowledge and management of those investments: they wanted the commissions on investments products but frankly, did not deserve them due to their poor knowledge and poor management skills.

Fourthly, there is a compensation risk that Advisors will not be rewarded for minimizing investment losses or for performing more detailed financial plans to reduce the likelihood of not meeting a retirement plan's goals, especially If the Advisory Firm's compensation only rewards new asset-gathering vs. taking care of the clients you have. I gathered assets but was more focused on client service than asset gathering. At times, I was in conflict with my firm for doing more client service than asset gathering, which can be lethal to a career as a financial Advisor.

The best way to deal with risks is (1) ensuring your Advisor has been trained adequately in all areas of financial planning and **(2) keeping** the Advisor accountable for their performance. **(3)** It also requires that you, the Advisory firm, and Advisor all **agree** and work toward mutual goals. The only person who can ensure this is all in sync is you, the client, and the purchaser of Investment Advisory services. (4) In my opinion ,you should read and keep up with investment trends and performance, so you can better keep the Advisory Firm and Advisor accountable to you.

I commonly read Barrons, Stockcharts.com, reviewed stocks in Vectorvest, read Business Week, The Economist, etc, plus the major economic and equity research of my firm. Forbes and Business Week can be good sources of information on companies you invest in. Sometimes I also read Investor's Business Daily. You don't need to read everything, but read about what you are invested in: those economies, companies, and products you have purchased. Vectorvest helped me identify new companies [equities] to invest in. Stockcharts.com identified what bond and equity markets were doing and, sometimes, opportunities of what sectors or companies were performing well, or lagging.

Managing the many risks outlined in these four bundles is very difficult and requires much training, experience, and discipline from firms, Advisors, and clients.

Most clients I met had lost money in equity markets and were trying to make up for it. Advisors sold annuities, took their money, and left the annuity unmanaged. Many lost up to 50% of their savings. [By the way, I never did that]. So carefully choose your Advisor, and always know what is happening in equity markets concerning volatility, the 50-day and 200-day moving averages, and what is happening in the banking sector.

Remember that when banks are sound and making money, when the $VIX index is around 20 [price] for its 50-day moving average, and when IWM, MDY, and SPY prices are all above their 50-day moving averages, the risk is lower, and this is a good time to invest. If client had lost money in prior equity downturns, I usually recommended 70% to 80% stocks, in the early stages of a bull market, to recover some of those losses. I gradually reduced one to two years down the road, to a normal asset allocation.

Advisors get sloppy after years of positive equity performance. Even Advisors forget about the risk of loss after years of gains. Advisors try to make money, but sometimes something else is needed. You should not be losing money in stocks or bonds. If that is a consistent theme in your investment accounts, find another Advisor.

Asset class performance
Among the various asset classes: cash, bonds, stocks, and alternative assets, Is constantly moving. That is why the advisors who monitor

performance of cash, bond, & equity markets and your investment port-folio, will be more likely to achieve consistent rate of returns, and out-perform other advisors. Find an advisor who carefully monitors bond and equity markets on a weekly basis.

There should always be an asset that is making money that you can invest in now. When stocks are falling, commodities can do well. Silver and gold can go up when interest rates rise, and bonds and stocks fall. Real estate sectors are booming at different times: housing and com-mercial real estate have different economic cycles. Even in equity market downturns, some stocks always become bargains because they either missed earnings, sales declined, or did not grow as much as forecast, etc. So, there are always opportunities to make money, even if acquiring large-cap value stocks that will take time to reap the gains. It would be great if you have an advisor who can recognize these opportunities.

Money constantly moves between these major asset classes of cash, bonds, stocks, alternative investments, real estate, and commodities. When interest rates rise as they have in the past 12-15 months, money moves out of long bonds. When equities fall, money moves out of stocks. When home prices are falling, money moves out of homes into other in-vestments. When stocks fall, money goes into commodities, especially oil and natural gas, from both equities and bonds. So, be confident, knowing there is always a way to make money. Make sure you have the kind of Advisor who can see opportunities throughout the major asset classes and is not stuck just trying to make money in equities and bonds with a buy and hold strategy.

Thoughts on fees and investments.
High fees represent a risk that you will not reach your financial goals be-cause too much of your returns were extracted from you by your advisor and their Advisory firm.

I offer the following advice on the investing and the costs of investing and when & why I choose certain investments at certain times:

1. **Due to the low costs of investing in ETFs [exchange-traded funds], you should invest in lower costs structures, like stocks and ETFs, and get rid of mutual funds** [unless this is the only way to invest in your company's 401k]. There are few Peter Lynch's and Warren Buffett's these days, and more money is passively managed. Most mutual funds have fees of 1.5% to 5% or more. Most of them underperform and are not worth your investment. If that is your only choice in your 401k, invest in those, but outside of your company investment 401k, try to use lower-cost structures, such as ETFs. Mutual funds are suitable for the fund companies who create them, but rarely are they the best vehicle for an investor who can qualify for better management and lower fees. Mutual funds were necessary when they offered diversification and professional management unavailable elsewhere but those days have passed. Mutual funds are dinosaurs currently being replaced by ETFs, lower costs, better diversification, and the replacement of below-average portfolio managers.

2. **I think about investments like this in terms of costs:** if you can invest in ETFs to get the exposure, return, and risk, use that, for example, an S&P 500 ETF, to have exposure to 500 of the largest stocks in the US and diversified multiple industries, and you have the lowest cost of investing. What could be better than that? Saving 1% or more on investment expenses is the same as earning 1% more from investment returns. Do everything you can to lower your fees. 1% per year accumulates over time. If you save 1% for 30 years, you will have substantially boosted your investment portfolio, its return, & its overall accumulation.

3. **I buy stocks when they outperform their index by 2% or more quarterly [a growth perspective]** or if their value is substantially more than equity markets currently value them [a value perspective]. Those two reasons are the primary reasons to buy stocks. And I put a 5% stops on them, so if they fall, [fast-growing stocks can drop quickly if their earnings slow], this will not significantly your portfolio. You purchase equities for overperformance, not for underperformance. Buying the S&P 500 index insures your portfolio against underperformance. You buy the "over performers" to get more returns while putting 5% stocks on them [possibly higher stops for these stocks] to manage investment risk. Additionally, in years where stocks are only appreciating 7% to 10% per year, investing in income-producing stocks, for example, oil companies that have a dividend, can improve your returns by 3-4% on your portfolio, and lower risk. That is a significant increase in years when performance is harder to achieve.

4. **I prefer to buy small-capitalization stocks only when they out perform the S&P 500.** It is better to pick and choose among small stocks that grow much faster than large companies but have more risk attached. I would use my firm's research or a software investment research program like Vectorvest.com, which can identify fast-growing companies. And I would put stops on these investments, between 5% and 10%. If you have a good advisor, get them to research small-cap stocks and get their recommendations on stops.

5. **I would own Berkshire Hathaway stock, BRK.A, in most investment accounts.** This investment offers the ability to outperform the S&P 500 stock index, with a superior portfolio managers. Overperformance in stocks comes from less diversified portfolios, as the more diversified you are, the more likely you have diversified away from the best performers. But you should diversify first. If

you have already invested in the S&P500 index, which insures against underperformance, this is the best way to over-perform, other than options on specific stocks.

6. **For international stocks, I would use my firm's research**, talk to your advisor, and do some research with Vectorvest.com. These stocks or ETFs are riskier than S&P 500 stocks and require risk management. Again I would use stops. I would look at the small-cap and international stocks, identify the best performers worth investing in, and then decide on an asset allocation based on my firm's research and the quality of the investment opportunities now available in small-cap and international stocks.

7. **I buy alternative investments when it diversifies risk**, have significant long-term capital gain potential, and when these investments can provide income when a client is distributing his assets [taking distributions monthly]. Suppose a client has done significant accumulation and is taking income. In that case, I think about an annuity to guarantee his ability to take income and get benefits that this investor cannot get from his investment account, such as income guarantees.

8. **I would regularly research the clean energy sector, low-carbon investing**, and research into using oil and coal more efficiently. This sector is popular & called the ESG sector, known as Environmental, Social, and Governance investing. Global investment into this sector was $501 billion in 2020, $755 billion in 2021, and $1.1 trillion in 2022, per Reuters. When solar power & wind turbine technology s increased by a magnitude of 10X where they started, that is when clean energy will produce more substantial investment returns, per Peter Thiel, in his book _Zero to One._ So far, the returns, compared to the investment, have been poor. The only successful clean energy company is Tesla. Look for companies that dominate

small niches first [also a suggestion of Peter Thiel, in his book **Zero to One**]. No one company is going to dominate global energy, a multi-trillion-dollar industry. However, one company will most likely lead in solar, wind, or new power generation. Look for public companies that dominate niches and have strong intellectual property protection, and real returns.

9. **I recommend buying options or futures when equity markets are shifting directions, firmly up or down.** Again, you may have to do this in your private investment accounts, not with an advisor. It would be best to do this with an advisor or expert. Make sure you have good investment research and know what you are doing. Know this is a risky move, but it can pay huge returns. These significant shifts show up in charts with 100-day and 200-day moving averages on the major indexes, such as the S&P 500 and Nasdaq 100 Composite, and are reflected clearly on charts, such as those by Stockcharts.com.

10. **Regarding investment publications, my favorites are Stockcharts.com, Barron's, and Investor's Business Daily.** And regarding software, I like Vectorvest.com, which analyzes 8000 stocks among small-cap, medium-cap, large-cap, and international companies and rates them. You can look at stocks by industry, by growth, etc. It helped me choose individual stocks and build portfolios.

My Advice on Your Financial Goals:

1. **Think about your lifetime financial goals.** What are they? Write them down. If you are married, discuss your plans with your spouse, and let each partner discuss their goals.

2. **Do you have automobile, home, and umbrella property insurance policies?** If not, start here and get quotes.

3. **Do you have health insurance at your work?** If not, get health insurance for yourself and your spouse. It would be best if your policies also cover children if you have children.

4. **Do you own life insurance yourself?** On your spouse? If you have a company policy, add one that you own for the primary wage-earner, then your spouse if you are married. If you have sufficient income and have saved money for retirement already, start over-funding your whole life policies.

5. **Have you started saving money?** Start with your company's 401k plan. If that is not available to you, open up a ROTH IRA. If you have both, start a taxable investment account.

6. **Before opening investment accounts, consider your long-term savings strategy and each possible investment account's tax consequences.** Do you have a 401K available to you? Have you opened up a ROTH IRA account? If you have a 401K available, save their first, primarily because a company match exists. If you do not have a 401K, open a ROTH IRA account and start maximum funding. Think about minimizing taxes wherever you can.

7. **Most clients should save more.** Saving more should lead to more honesty with your advisors. They sometimes lie to make up for losses and inadequate savings. They offer more returns than possible to try to make your plan work. You intend to save more money, and most advisors do try to help you meet your goals.

8. **Be wary of advisors who say they can earn more than 10% annualized investment return for the long term.** If you factor in 4% inflation and some investment expenses, achieving more than a 5.5% to 7% rate of return over the long term is challenging. A 7% real rate of return may be achievable when equity markets are going

up, but what is a reasonable rate of return when markets are going down? This rarely gets discussed.

9. **Most advisors should utilize risk management products more.** It would be best to have stops [sell orders] on all your bond and equity investing positions. You cannot put a stop to a mutual fund. So, it would be better to own individual stocks and equity positions carefully chosen by research and put 3% stops on all bond positions and 5% stops on all equity positions. Then you can avoid the 15% to 25% equity market drops and retire earlier with more money. Isn't that why you are reading this book?

10. **Clients should keep their advisors accountable.** Most do not. Due to time factors, busy careers, and busy mothers and fathers, many investment advisors get away with murder, at least murder to an investment portfolio, by losing big when equity markets go down. It is your money. Keep your Advisor accountable with monthly or quarterly meetings to discuss investment portfolio performance. Find another advisor if your Advisor will not have investment meetings to discuss performance.

11. **What do you know about investments?** Ask your advisor questions about any investment that you do not understand. It would be best to learn about investments as you buy them, to be sure you understand their risk and return characteristics. Keep learning about investments: read books about the areas of investing you find most interesting, such as small-cap stocks, etc. Do your best to learn more about investing, as knowledge reduces your risk of loss, and may eliminate biases.

12. **Learn more about risk management products** to help you avoid losses in your investment accounts. Ensure that you understand stop losses/sell orders and options such as buying calls on stocks

you own or selling calls on stocks you own, to gain additional income, say when equity markets are falling.

Whether you choose to move assets from a 401k or IRA to your firm or a new firm:

1. **Your investment choices should be broader and of higher quality,** with more excellent opportunities to invest, representing more risk profiles, and among all the asset classes of cash, bonds, stocks & equity investments, and REITs, real estate investment trusts, that investment in a variety of real estate.

2. **You can increase the quality of your investments and lower your investing expenses**. For example, your new investment advisor may charge you a flat 1% fee, while your retirement assets at your company have mutual funds with costs of 1.5% to over 2%. Lower investing expenses will help you gain more returns and help you reach your investing goals.

3. **You benefit from having your retirement assets in one place**, with one advisor overseeing all your investments. It is better to have one advisor managing your money than to make your life more complex with multiple advisors. And then hold them accountable for their performance. But that is your decision.

4. **You have a more experienced advisor or team**, with experts in investments, insurance, taxes, financial and estate planning, with more transparency, and more accountability.

   Make sure that moving your assets to an advisor [or one advisor] is best for you. Do that if the advisory firm has great research, investments, insurance, and financial planning expertise, and offers the broadest range of investment products, including alternative investments. Will they allow you access to their research?

Storytime

Now the story is about you. About who you select as an Advisor. And what financial plans you make together, how you invest, and how well you address insurance and investing risks. Whether you choose an Advisor who knows how to avoid investment losses, with the investment managers your Advisor picks as portfolio managers, how well they perform. How well do you accomplish estate planning? How well do you and the Advisor review your retirement plan? How consistently is the Advisor accountable for investment results and has a new strategy if the current one is not working?

I practiced Advisor led with my clients [meaning I led these processes after discussions with clients] but always sought their input and agreement before implementing any strategy. I always showed the respect that it was the client's goals and money we were working with. It doesn't work when the client wants to lead all discussions. Clients lead with goals and concerns, and Advisors respond with strategies to be reviewed and agreed to by the client before implementation. I think this relationship is mutual, respectful, and has clear boundaries. That is the only way I see this relationship working.

I have given you all the tools you need to utilize a Financial Advisor/or Financial Advisor Team successfully and build your wealth. What you do with these tools is up to you. I wish you the very best in achieving all your financial goals.

About the Author

Brent writes to share his experience as a financial advisor, to be helpful to investors with advisors, and assist them in growing their wealth, and to educate investors who do not have a financial advisor, so they can make the most informed financial decisions.

He holds a Bachelor of Science in Business Administration from the University of Nebraska, with majors in Accounting, Business Administration, and Economics. Brent earned an MBA from the University of Houston, with honors, emphasizing Finance and Marketing. He earned the Chartered Financial Analyst and Certified Financial Planner designations.

This book opens up the world of advisory firms and their advisors, and how they act. It seeks to help investors hold advisors accountable, and build a strong relationship with their advisor that serves the client.